Every Heart
has a gift

Every Heart
has a gift

a collaboration by
Janet C. Bernstein

of

Every Heart Project

Other books by this publisher:
Pizza on the Floor, 2016 Every Heart Has a Story, 2017
The Savvy Girl Media's Guide to Branding, 2018
The Starting Over Toolbox, 2018
The New Rules of the Sisterhood, 2019

ISBN: 979-8-68-224129-3

Cover design by Janet C. Bernstein, Intuitive Coach & Healer
Copyediting by Janet C. Bernstein, Intuitive Coach & Healer
Proofreading by Ariana C. Scott
Printed in the United States of America

Dedication

This book is dedicated to the hearts around the world who have not yet found the courage to share their stories or gifts. When you are ready, the world is waiting. You matter. Your story is not over yet.

Shine your light.

The Gifts

The Gift of Freedom

by Janet C. Bernstein

> *Freedom lies in the ability to express yourself with love.*
> *Don't hold yourself captive with fear by trying to impress*
> *others with an illusion.*
>
> ~ *Unknown*

We were nestled into a cozy leather booth in a busy brunch restaurant, patiently waiting for our server to take our order. We had not eaten since the night before and I was beginning to feel irritated because of it. The sounds of silverware clinking together, and plates being harshly tossed in the kitchen distracted me from the sudden change in the field of energy around me. I was instantly drawn to her presence across the room, knowing I was being given information to help her or deliver a message. I sighed heavily. This was not really the part of my calling I loved; delivering news to a stranger in the middle of my Saturday morning when all I wanted to do was order my avocado toast and over-medium eggs. *"If only I could just be a normal person,"* I thought to myself, as I sat my menu down on the table.

"What's up, baby?" my husband asked. *"Are you ready to order?"*

I tilted my head slightly and sighed again. *"Can you order me the avocado toast with over-medium eggs and a side of hollandaise? I have to go talk to someone."* I said.

He knew. We had been married just a few years, but he had seen that look in my eyes before, and he was familiar with my gifts. As I stood up from the booth, I made my way over to a woman who worked for the restaurant. She was olive skinned, petite, with curly black hair tied back in a ponytail. She seemed agitated and focused, until she saw me approach. *"Hello,"* I began, knowing I was about to potentially scare her or surprise her with what I was going to say. *"I have a message for you. You have been through something very tragic recently, perhaps you lost someone close to you? The message is that you are strong and courageous, and you are supposed to move forward. Stop standing still. It is okay to mourn what has been lost, but you still have so much to look forward to, and ending your life is not an option. You are loved and you are worthy."*

As I stopped talking, the woman's eyes filled with tears and she hugged me. She thanked me for the message and even shared with me that she had prayed to God that very morning and asked for a sign to let her know an answer to an especially important question. She told me that I delivered her answer. I smiled, trying to hold back tears myself. I was humbled, but also exhausted. Every time I tap into the energy field of another person to do this, I feel zapped afterward. It reminds me of spending hours in the Texas summer sun, only to come home, shower, and pass out early for bed.

I came back to our booth, where my husband was eagerly awaiting the story. He loved to hear about the things I saw or felt, and always supported my calling, even if it was not considered 'normal' for many people. I briefly shared what happened, and he sat listening in awe. *"So, what do you think she's been through?"* he asked, when I told him of a recent loss. *"Oh, she lost a child,"* I immediately answered, then realized she did not share that with me. It was just one of the things I knew. I smiled. These gifts are unexplainable to many people, but such a blessing for those I try to help. A few minutes later, our brunch arrived, and we continued with our Saturday.

I have hundreds of these stories, all dating back to my childhood. I have blurted out things that no one possibly thought I could know, all from tragedies to triumphs, and have blown away even the biggest of skeptics. I listen to my intuition and the divine guidance around me, and I am obedient to my gifts. It has helped me avoid relationships, circumvent career fails, choose friends wisely, and help dozens of women entrepreneurs launch their businesses and overcome mindset blocks and challenges.

But I did not always embrace my gifts.

For many years, I hid my incredible talents from everyone. I downplayed how I knew things, by simply laughing it off and saying I had a photographic memory (which I also have) or just got lucky when I guessed the exact number of jelly beans in the jar in third grade. I remember one year in elementary school when I had a vision of winning a poster contest for recycling, and I had a clear image of the winning poster. I did not think much of it until a few days after my vision, our school announced this poster contest. I recreated the poster I saw in my vision, down to the little plastic cups strategically hot-glued all over the board with little bits of trash dangling off the sides. I won first place and received a little blue ribbon. The image of that ribbon was drawn in my diary a week before.

One time I told a teacher about a vision I had seen about her family, and apparently, I was a little too close for her comfort. She immediately crossed her arms and asked me how I knew what I knew. She closed her energy field and blocked me out, which was the first time I experienced that reaction. Unfortunately, it was not the last time, and that still happens from time to time. When I became an adult, I stopped sharing my gifts with others. I rarely used them, and I kept my visions and messages to myself for many years. It was not until I met my second husband, Harold, that I finally opened up and shared these unique gifts. I remember being on our first date, and I began receiving Divine Downloads (which is how I describe the messages I receive.) I could see various images and I began delivering what I was seeing. I did not hold back, which really surprised me, because I had not shared such things with anyone in so long. As I kept talking, I watched the doubt and uncertainty melt from his face. He was blown away. He was touched. His energy transformed right before my very eyes, and I think I possibly fell in love with him that night. He told me I was incredibly intuitive and 'spot on.' He then began to ask me question after question about my gifts and abilities. He was fascinated, intrigued, and wanted to know more. We talked for hours about my childhood and how I discovered my gifts. I shared my experiences of being turned away from my church following my own divorce, and how I was dedicating my gifts to my corporate career and coaching fast-pitch girls' softball, which was how we initially were connected. I admitted that I was squandering my gifts in a sense, and not using them as much as I should be. For the first time, someone was encouraging me to share those gifts and to not be ashamed of them. He saw the magical sparkle in my eyes that comes when I am helping someone and allowing the gifts to flow through me. He saw my love for healing. He saw me.

I wish I could say I confidently stepped into my purpose after that, without doubt or reservation.

But that would be a big, fat lie.

I hesitated.
I doubted myself.
I feared criticism.
I feared judgment.
I feared failure.
I feared success.

I hid in that 'spiritual closet' for several more years, until I was in the middle of a coaching session with a client, who was sitting across from me in my home office. We had already completed several sessions, but today was different. She was having a breakthrough, and I was receiving Divine Downloads the entire time. I began to relay the messages I was receiving, without questioning whether it was 'safe' to do so. I watched her facial expressions change as she realized my true abilities emerge. She was speechless. I suddenly realized that I had allowed myself to speak this truth without holding back, something I had not done in years.

I finally stopped talking, and broke the awkward silence with, *"so yeah, I sort of have some intuitive gifts I use in my coaching business."* I eagerly awaited her response, praying it did not mean she would jump up from my office and run out, never to see me again, telling everyone we knew that I was some crystal-ball-loving gypsy. She stayed silent a few minutes before breaking down into tears. She then told me she knew this was the reason she was drawn to me and my coaching practice, and how she was so relieved to know my gifts were God-given.

God-given.

I had never heard anyone tell me that before. Most of the people who found out about my gifts were hesitant to connect them to God, and I am sad to admit I have spent many hours defending my faith because of this. I had a dear friend tell me if I was 'hearing things,' then it was likely that the devil was whispering in my ear. Another acquaintance quoted some scriptures warning me of fortune-telling. I am not a huge fan of arguing, so I just allow people to speak their truth or beliefs, and I simply listen without feeling the need to interrupt or explain. But over time, that equated to silence, resentment, and eventually, dimming my own light. I allowed my fear of being judged to overpower my desire to shine brightly and help those in my charge.

In August 2019, I decided it was time to come out of that spiritual closet. I was ready. I released the fear and finally revealed my new title, "Intuitive Coach and Healer." I recorded a live video to explain my new focus and come clean about the gifts that led me to this place. I did not hold back. I was finally speaking my truth.

The support was mixed from most of the friends and family in my life. The reactions ranged from, *"I knew it all along!"* to *"that totally makes sense now."* I also heard from a few who chose to let me know that using that word, "intuitive" would introduce me to some "crazy people." I laughed. I think I AM part of the crazy people to which he was referring. And I am okay with that.

These gifts *are* God-given.

My purpose to help others heal and grow is divinely inspired and guided. If I hide and dim my light, I deprive others of a gift I am called to use and share. If I embrace my gifts, shine my light, and speak my truth, I receive the greatest gift of all…

Freedom.

More About Janet:

Janet Bernstein is an Intuitive Coach and Healer, as well as a best-selling author who helps women overcome fears, embrace their authenticity, and break through mindset blocks to achieve financial freedom. Janet left a 17-year career in corporate insurance to pursue her dream of teaching women around the world to step into their purpose and unleash their full potential. She is the founder of Every Heart Project, a heart centered, membership-based women's organization that provides monthly events, masterminds, mentoring, workshops, and purpose-filled retreats. Janet's sixth book *The New Rules of the Sisterhood* was featured on ABC's Good Morning Texas.

Contact Janet:

Website: www.janetcbernstein.com
Website: www.everyheartproject.com

The Gift of Encouragement

by Lawrencina Mason Oramalu

Fear, Faith, and My Future

When I was growing up, people used to always ask me, *"What do you want to do when you grow up?"* I remember wanting to become a doctor until I realized I was afraid of blood. While my fear of blood prevented me from pursuing a career as a medical doctor, I have tried to live a life where I can bring a different kind of healing to people. I am not equipped to bring physical healing to people, but I would like to believe that I am able to help heal broken hearts and broken spirits. I cannot repair fractured ligaments, but I can offer people a prescription for their fractured relationships, fractured confidence, and fractured faith because I am a living witness that faith in God can heal a broken heart and a broken spirit, and I believe God has called me to let others know He can do it for them too.

As a child, I was afraid to look at blood, and as an adult, I have tried to stay clear of anything that would require me to work with blood. Despite my fears, I now realize that the job God has called me to pursue is connected to blood. If you look at my resume, this may not make since because you will not see any professional titles that relate to occupations that work with blood. However, I can now look at my life and see how my job is absolutely connected to blood. The blood of Jesus Christ saved me from sin. Christ died on the cross so that I could be saved. The blood that saved me gives me hope, joy, and peace, and I have always tried to share hope and encouragement with others. In John 10:10, the Bible says,

> *The thief does not come except to steal, and to kill, and to destroy. I have come that they may have life, and that they may have it more abundantly.*

Throughout my life, Satan has tried to steal my joy and kill my spirits, and I am thankful that God is able to restore and heal. As God restored my joy and healed my spirits, I want to do the same for others.

When I think about the question, *"What gift or gifts do you possess and how have they changed your life or the lives of others?"* I think about Romans 12:6-8 which says,

> *We have different gifts, according to the grace given to each of us. If your gift is prophesying, then prophesy in accordance with your faith; if it is serving, then serve; if it is teaching, then teach; if it is to encourage, then give*

encouragement; if it is giving, then give generously; if it is to lead, do it diligently; if it is to show mercy, do it cheerfully. 🙶 *(NIV)*

Hopefully, we can all see our gifts in this scripture, and if I had to pick a primary gift from this list, I would pick encouragement.

I Trust the Plans God Has for Me

I remember I used to feel bad about having moved around to different jobs throughout my career. Major life changes caused me to move to different states and start all over again. In 1995, I moved from Houston, Texas to Minnesota because I was going through a divorce. In 2015, I moved from Minnesota back to Texas because my job had been eliminated. Change is never easy, and it can especially be difficult when you find yourself having to start all over again in a new state.

After I arrived in Texas in 2015, my career took several twists and turns. Some people might look at my resume and conclude that I am not a very stable or reliable person. While there are some people who can boast that they have been at a job for 5 years, 10 years, 15 years, or 20 years, that definitely does not describe me. If you looked at my life over the past five years, you might scratch your head and wonder if I know what I am doing. Honestly, I do not always know what I am doing, but God does.

In 2015, I left my job as Director of Equity and Diversity for a school district in Minnesota. When my family relocated to Texas, I was unemployed for over a year. I worked as a part-time bookstore clerk and then I worked as a reception at my husband's new business. I left the clinic when I found a job as a program manager for a nonprofit. I later found a director level job at a community college. Some people might look at my resume with skepticism and wonder why I moved around so much. To the human eye, it might not make sense, but in God's eyes, everything makes sense. In Jeremiah 29:11, the Bible says:

> For I know the plans I have for you," declares the Lord, "plans to prosper you and not to harm you, plans to give you hope and a future.

Despite what my circumstances or my resume might look like or what professional title I have, I have decided to trust God to order my steps. I have decided to use my gift of encouragement wherever I am and however I can. My faith and commitment to turn my future over to the Lord is echoed by the words of former President Jimmy Carter who once said.

> I have one life and one chance to make it count for something. My faith demands that I do whatever I can, wherever I am, whenever I can, for as long as I can with whatever I have, to try to make a difference.

Hence, whether the Lord places me in the medical field, legal field, business field, education field, technology, or public sector, I will do what I can to make a difference. Whether I am leading, following, serving, writing, teaching, selling books, making coffee, making copies, or answering phones, I will do it all to the glory of the Lord. I no longer get caught up in the title I have because just like Dr. Martin Luther King, Jr. said, we can all be great if we serve.

> Everybody can be great...because anybody can serve. You don't have to have a college degree to serve. You don't have

to make your subject and verb agree to serve. You only need a heart full of grace. A soul generated by love. 🙴

Doctor of Encouragement

As someone who loves school and considers herself a lifelong learner, I sometimes wish I could go back to school for my doctorate degree. No, I would not go to medical school because I am still a little afraid of blood. Although the Lord allowed me to earn my Juris Doctorate, I still think about getting another degree. Since I have spent so many years working in education, I would love to get my Doctorate in Education. Well, up to this point, the time and circumstances have not been right for me to go back to school. Nevertheless, the good news is that all is not lost. I have realized that I already have a doctorate. I am awarding myself a Doctorate of Encouragement, so I am declaring myself to be a pseudo-medical doctor.

Lawrencina, the pseudo-ophthalmologists. Ophthalmologist help people with their vision. When we see an ophthalmologist, they will help us figure out what corrective action we need to take so that we can see better. We may need to invest in some corrective lenses to help us see clearly. Well, throughout my life, I have tried to help people see the potential they have inside of them. They might look in the mirror and not see the greatness that is inside of them. They might see their past mistakes. They may look at their current situation and not see what is possible. They might see themselves as unworthy, unqualified, or unprepared because of what someone else has told them or what they have told themselves. They might feel insignificant or insecure. As a pseudo ophthalmologist, I want to help people see their worth. I want to help them see their value. They may look in the mirror and see their flaws, but I want them to see themselves as Christ sees them. I want them to know that in Psalm 139:14, God says that we are *"fearfully and wonderfully made."*

Some people need corrective lenses so they can see clearly, and I want to help them. I do not want people to have blurred vision. I do not want them to allow negative people, experiences, or negative self-talk to blur their vision about who they really are. I want to help people look at their life through God's corrective lenses. Through my new company, Soar2BMore, I facilitate different types personal growth and development workshops. In the session, It's Time to Bloom: Discover Your Purpose, Passion, and Potential, I facilitate a series on John Maxwell's book, The 15 Invaluable Laws of Growth, which covers several important laws such as the Law of the Mirror, which teaches people that *"You must see value in yourself to add value to others."* We also go over the Law of Pain which teaches us that *"Good management of bad experiences leads to great growth."* Essentially, in this life, we will have bad experiences, but we do not need to allow these bad experiences to discourage us or deny us from stepping forward towards fulfilling our potential. We need to continue to see the potential and greatness inside of us, despite the pain we might encounter on the journey. In addition to the personal growth and development sessions I offer, I also recently authored a book, Look Up, Step Up, and Soar: Lessons of Hope, Restoration, and Transformation, in which I encourage the reader to keep their eyes focused on God's promises and not on our problems. As the pseudo-ophthalmologist, I can encourage people to keep looking up to God and not look down at their problems.

Lawrencina, the pseudo-obstetrician. Obstetricians work with women to help them deliver a healthy baby, and throughout my life, I have tried to help nurture the potential that is inside of people and to help them give birth to their dreams. I believe that everyone has potential inside of them. In his book, <u>The 15 Invaluable Laws of Growth</u>, John Maxwell says, *"God's gift to us is our potential, and our gift to God is developing it."* I believe this with all my heart, and I am committed to helping other people develop their potential and give birth to their hopes and dreams. To give birth to their dreams, they need to overcome their fears. Is childbirth painful? Yes. Is the pain worth it? Absolutely! We just need to push through the fear. In her book, <u>Abundance Now</u>, Lisa Nichols provides advice on how to push through the fear.

> *To step inside your greatness and begin using the genius that has been uniquely given to you – something I call "living in your light" – you are going to have to allow yourself to be free of old constraints and give yourself permission to stand in your power. What does that look like? Standing in your power is when you are committed to pushing past any negative self-talk, rising above your own fears, and evicting any disempowering thoughts or chatter that does not support your highest calling and greatest service.*

As a pseudo-obstetrician I want to encourage, equip, and empower women to rise up, step into their light, and give birth to their dreams.

Lawrencina, the pseudo-radiologists. Radiologists examine people's bodies to see if there are broken bones or if there is a something inside our bodies that is causing problems. Maybe there is a cancer inside that is spreading to other parts of our body. Maybe there is blockage inside that is preventing blood from flowing the way it should. I want to help people identify what is in their minds or their hearts that is creating blocks in their lives. What is preventing them from being able to take that next step on their journey to fulfill their potential and be all that God has called them to be? Do they have some unforgiveness, anger, resentment, or jealousy inside that is blocking the flow of God's blessings? Do we need to allow God to reach inside and perform surgery on those things and purge our hearts? Do we need to purge our minds from thinking about things that are not pleasing to Him and do not give Him glory? In Romans 12:2, the Bible tells us that we need to renew our minds.

> "Do not conform to the pattern of this world but be transformed by the renewing of your mind. Then you will be able to test and approve what God's will is—his good, pleasing and perfect will."

I want to continually renew my mind and help others to renew theirs so that we can be sure that we are able to live out God's perfect will for our lives. In my book, I talk about how the Lord had to help me to remove unforgiveness from my heart so it could stop weighing me down.

Bringing Things Back from the Dead

God is so awesome that He can use our weaknesses in one area to be a strength in another area. I already admitted that I am afraid of blood and therefore could not pursue a real medical career. I had to settle for being a pseudo-doctor by awarding myself a Doctorate of Encouragement. I also do not have a green thumb, so I am not naturally good with taking care of flowers and plants. Well, even though I am not naturally gifted at taking care of plants, I now know that it is possible to bring some plants back to life that once looked dead.

When I used to work at the University of Minnesota, my mother thought that I needed a plant in my office, so she bought me one. She knew that I did not have a green thumb so she wanted to buy me something that I could not kill. I remember being so proud of myself for keeping this plant for years. Even when I neglected it by forgetting to water it, all I had to do was pour a little water in it, and it would perk back up. This showed me that the plant was not really dead. There was life still in the plant. It just needed a little love and attention. As a pseudo-horticulturalist, when I look at people who society might write off as worthless or dead, I still see life. All they need is a little water. They are thirsty for hope, love, encouragement, and attention. We have students in classrooms that are like my plant. Some might feel neglected, forgotten, misunderstood, or targeted. Some may feel neglected at home. Others might feel neglected by a system that has written them off because of their race, ethnicity, zip code, socioeconomic status, or gender. We may have teenagers or adults that have made some mistakes in their past and society tells them that they are a mistake. Society may not want to give them another chance or a helping hand. We may look at our circumstances, and through our human eye's, our life might look dead. We have lost a job or a relationship, but our lives are not over. It is only a chapter. Just like I was able to bring my plant back to life by pouring water in it, so too we can bring life back into our people. We just need to add a little water of hope and encouragement.

Well, even though I am not naturally gifted at taking care of plants, an experience I had trying to revive a dead plant helped me realize the power of a little love and encouragement.

Our Nation Needs a Doctor

Racism, hate, and unconscious bias are cancers that are spreading throughout our nation and must be stopped. If we do not address the spread, these cancers will continue to cripple the growth and development of our nation. I have personally witnessed the damage that diseases and broken ligaments can have on a person's physical body and ability to function. Years ago, my brave sister, Johnnie Ann Crawford, was diagnosed with breast cancer and had to go through chemotherapy, but I thank God that she is now a proud breast cancer survivor. Although she was a tiny baby at birth, only weighing 2 pounds, her strength and resilience has never been small. She has continued to grow and develop throughout her childhood and adult life. In addition to battling cancer, she has had several hip replacements because the imbalanced weight of her body weakened her hips. The hip replacements were supposed to strengthen her body so she could walk without pain. Similarly, our nation needs a hip replacement. We are one body and one nation, and we should not allow labels to divide and cripple us. Unfortunately, we have allowed the weight of racism, hatred, politics, and division to erode the hips of our country. Our failure to address these ailments has crippled us and decreased our ability to walk together as one nation. If we allow racism, hate, and division to permeate throughout our communities and our nation, we will continue to limp along and not live up to our full potential. Our hip bone needs to be replaced so that our body can be healed.

I believe that God not only wants me to use my gift of encouragement to help individuals and organizations live up to their God-given potential, but I believe He also wants me to try to encourage everyone to commit to helping our nation live up to its potential. I admit this will not be an easy task, because I have questioned whether it is possible.

Lately I have felt deep sadness, pain, and discouragement as I have watched the tragic events unfold over the summer with the death of George Floyd and others. Nevertheless, while I have had moments of discouragement and despair, my heart and mind get renewed when I turn to God's word. When I look at Ezekiel chapter 37, I see a story like what we are experiencing in our nation. This chapter describes how a valley of dry bones is transformed into living bones. Right now, I feel like our nation is full of dry, damaged, and cracked bones, kind of like my sister's damaged hip bone.

While my sister's hip was recently repaired, I do not necessarily feel as confident about the likelihood our nation's bones can be repaired. Despite my temporary doubts and despair, I find hope and encouragement in Ezekiel 37, where a similar question was asked. In verse 3, Ezekiel asked, *"Son of man, can these dry bones live?"* The bones were a symbol of the people of Israel, and verse 11 says, *"They say, 'Our bones are dried up and our hope is gone."* Although I initially felt hopeless about the state of our nation, the more I read my Bible, the more hopeful I become. In verse 14, it says, *"I will put my Spirit in you, and you will live."* This verse can be applied to the current need of our nation. We need the Holy Spirit to breathe life, hope, and encouragement throughout our nation because it is full of dry, divided bones. We are divided along political party. We are divided among race and ethnicity. We are divided along economic status. We are divided among religious affiliation. There are so many labels that are keeping us divided, but a divided nation will fall, and if we do not do something to try to unify our nation, then we will not be able to live up to our potential. I am hoping and praying that our nation's story can follow the progression of the story in Ezekiel chapter 37 because verse 22 says, *"they will never again be two nations or be divided into two kingdoms"*, and verse 26 says, *"I will make a covenant of peace with them."* I pray we can be one nation and that we will not allow our differences to continue to divide us and keep our bones dry. I pray we can find peace in our land and everyone will be treated justly and fairly.

I hope and pray that one day, everyone will feel we are living out the true meaning of the Declaration of Independence, which says:

> *We hold these truths to be self-evident, that all men are created equal, that they are endowed by their Creator with certain unalienable rights, that among these are Life, Liberty, and the pursuit of Happiness.*

If our nation believes that all men and women are created equal, then we must treat all men and women equal. We must not have educational, health, economic, and criminal justice systems that produce racial disparities. If we see injustice against a group in our society, may we all rise up and speak up. Let us not only remember the words of the Declaration of Independence, but let us also remember the words of Dr. Martin Luther King, Jr. who said:

> ***Injustice anywhere** is a **threat to justice everywhere.** We are caught in an inescapable network of mutuality, tied in a single garment of destiny. Whatever affects one directly, affects all indirectly.*

I believe we are all connected. We are one body and one nation that needs to be healed, and throughout the rest of my life, I will try to point people to the ultimate doctor and healer, God the Father. But I will also use my Doctorate of Encouragement to encourage people to strive to help our nation live up to its potential. May we all work to stop the bleeding and start the healing. May our dry bones by healed, and our hip bone repaired.

My Official Title Does Not Matter

Sometimes we are tempted to judge our lives based on our official title. We may judge ourselves based on whether we are a doctor, a lawyer, a teacher, a judge, a business owner, politician, police officer, cosmetologist, cashier, mechanic, housekeeper, receptionist or whatever profession we end up pursuing, but the truth is that it is not our title or profession that really matters. In the end, what matters is whether we are using our gifts, skills, and talents to make a difference in the lives of others. Are we trying to make the world a better place?

Since I was afraid of blood, I did not try to pursue a medical profession, but I did end up pursuing a degree in another helping profession. I thought I could help "save the world" and help people by obtaining a law degree. Although I finished law school, I never officially served as a practicing attorney. My mother sometimes gets a little frustrated because she wants to see me working in a legal setting. My husband also wonders why I spent all that time and money to go to law school if I was not going to use the degree. Well, I do not think it was a total waste. Lawyers are trained in how to interpret the law, how to write, how to persuade, how to think critically, and how to be an effective advocate. They try to encourage or persuade a judge or jury to reach a certain decision. While I am not a traditional practicing attorney, I am working to interpret the law and trying to encourage people to reach a decision. Instead of interpreting the Constitution and other laws, I am seeking to interpret biblical laws and encourage people to see themselves as Christ sees them. Hence, whatever job title I have, the main title that I will carry wherever life takes me, is Child of God, Believer, Christ-follower,

Daughter of the King, and my main responsibility and gift I will seek to use and develop is the gift of encouragement.

So, my resume might not look very impressive to some people. It might make me look unreliable and unstable since I have moved around to various jobs but thank goodness I no longer look to the world for approval and validation. I now look to the Lord for approval. I rely on God to order my steps and direct my path. My career path might look unstable, but I trust in someone who is stable. I trust in God whose thoughts and plans are higher than mine. I will continue to do whatever He says. I will continue to spread hope and encouragement. I will continue to try to be a light and to allow the Lord to use me to help heal broken hearts and broken spirits. I will allow Him to use me to repair fractured confidence and faith as well as help people give birth to their hopes and dreams. I will continue to encourage people to Soar2BMore and be all that God created them to be.

More About Lawrencina:

In a world that is sometimes consumed with messages of hopelessness, fear, anxiety, and negativity, Lawrencina chooses to spread a message of hope, love, faith, and encouragement. One of her favorite scriptures is Romans 8:28 which says, "And we know that all things work together for good to them that love God, to them who are the called according to his purpose." Lawrencina believes that her purpose in life is to encourage others and help them to reach their God-given potential.

Like most people, throughout her life, Lawrencina has experienced highs and lows, but when she found herself in the valleys of life, she stood on God's promises in Isaiah 40:31 - "but those who **hope** in the Lord will **renew** their strength. They will **soar** on wings like eagles; they will run and not grow weary; they will walk and not be faint." Since God blessed Lawrencina to soar out of her valleys, she decided to start Soar2bMore, an organization designed to encourage, educate, empower, and equip people with the tools to reach their God-given potential. Lawrencina seeks to fulfill the organization's mission through writing, speaking, and teaching. Her first book, Look Up, Step Up, and Soar: Lessons of Hope, Restoration, and Transformation will be published in 2020, and she regularly blogs on her website at www. soar2bmore.com/blog.

In 2020, Lawrencina became a certified John Maxwell speaker and trainer which means she can deliver keynote speeches, as well as workshops or short or long-term trainings utilizing several of John Maxwell's award-winning leadership and personal development books. Lawrencina loves to speak and welcomes the opportunity to share words of encouragement to audiences of any size.

Lawrencina first started public speaking as a child at her church home, Metropolitan Missionary Baptist Church in Kansas City, Missouri. She is grateful for the love, nurturing, and encouragement she received from her Pastor, Reverend Dr. Wallace S. Hartsfield, Sr., and her church family. Her love for writing and public speaking started at Metropolitan, where she wrote essays for the annual Black History Month oratorical contest and spoke in Easter and Christmas programs. Lawrencina is eternally grateful for the support and encouragement she received from her biological and church family.

Lawrencina earned her BA in Political Science and Policy Studies from Rice University in Houston, Texas, her MA in Public Affairs from the University of Minnesota's Humphrey School of Public Affairs, and her JD from William Mitchell College of Law in St. Paul, Minnesota. She is married to Dr. Frank Oramalu, and the proud mother of three children – Bobbie Ngozi, Obinna Emmanuel, and Frank Ikechukwu. She is blessed to have both parents, William Lawrence and Reverend Barbara Fountain-Mason, alive to celebrate with her as she enters this new chapter of her life as a writer and speaker.

You can learn more about Lawrencina and Soar2BMore at www.soar2bmore.com

The Gift of Appreciation

by Kim Peake

> *Everyone has a gift, but not every person recognizes what his or her gift is. Being able to identify it is the key to fulfilling the unique purpose of your life. However, don't confuse a gift with talent. Anyone can learn a talent, but a gift is something you're born with.*
>
> ~ Steve Harvey

Some people never stop and ask themselves, *"What is my gift? How do I know what my gifts are?"* Many people spend their lives trying to build a career in which they do not excel or are passionate about. Often, we get stuck in a place where we feel too comfortable, and we stop growing and challenging ourselves. This is where imposter syndrome may develop. The psychological idea of imposter syndrome is described as a severe inadequacy and self-doubt that can leave many strong women fearing they will be exposed as a fraud. It can affect anyone, regardless of their success. Many times, I have been my own worst enemy, hiding behind my fears. Worrying about the "what ifs" held me back.

For as long as I can remember, I always have been interested in the idea of our natural gifts. Unfortunately, many people in this world never discover their true calling and how they can serve the higher good for all. Natural gifts come in all shapes and sizes, unique to everyone. Each one of us carries within us certain gifts and attributes that positively contribute to society.

Here are questions to ask yourself when trying to discover your abilities and talents:

What do you feel your natural gifts are?

How can you positively contribute to society?

Many people I know have suppressed their amazing skills and talents over time, and so once they want to be cracked open, it can be exceedingly difficult to figure out what their true gifts are. However, I know from personal experience that figuring out your calling and what fulfills you is one of the most important things that you can do for yourself and others. The emergence of these gifts allows you to have the best life possible. Oftentimes, if we are not living in the present, our gifts will never come to life. Our God-given gifts are not supposed to be a detriment to us, but a reality that is always growing and learning.

> *Have no fear of perfection - you'll never reach it.*
> *-Salvador Dali*

Our gifts are things that we are naturally drawn to and can cultivate easily. We enjoy serving others through our gifts without much thought, as it just should come naturally to us. At times, we often take these gifts for granted without even realizing they do so. So many people think that their gifts are not special and assume that the things they are extremely talented in are easy for others as well. This is not the case much of the time. Gifts often emerge when we are honest with ourselves and true to the ones we love. When we seek inspiration, we often will find our gifts through discovering what brings us the most joy. What comes easily and lights us up inside is usually a key indicator of the natural gifts we possess. Once we can identify some of our gifts, we are given the opportunity to truly live our best life. The successes in life we experience often are correlated to our gifts. However, we must figure out how we can best utilize our gifts to help others and bring joy to ourselves.

> *Each person is born with a gift. Our call is to find it and care for it. The ultimate purpose of the gift is to exercise the heart into inhabiting its aliveness. For the covenant of life is not just to stay alive, but to stay in our aliveness. And staying in aliveness depends on opening the heart and keeping it open.*
>
> ~ Mark Nepo

Since the time I was little, I have always wanted to teach and give the gift of knowledge to others. From the time I was a little girl, I always wanted to help others learn information that would allow them to better themselves. I come from an extensive line of strong, intelligent, hard-working women who were able to better themselves despite their hardships and circumstances. These women worked tirelessly every day to be able to provide their children with more opportunities than they were given. My family lineage has several educators, doctors, engineers, attorneys, and entrepreneurs that worked hard to utilize their gifts to support their families and find fulfillment in their careers. I was blessed with amazing role models as a child, and I knew I wanted to serve others just as they had done with generations before me. My gift of teaching was born.

People are often blessed with more than one gift, and it is their responsibility to maximize these gifts to serve as many people as possible on this earth during a lifetime. In addition to having the gift of teaching, my main gift is the ability to find the light and positivity in everything. My career for the past 16 years has been dedicated to students. I have served as an educator, counselor, administrator, tutor, consultant, and charity board member, and mentor. Teaching my students and being able to "light them up about learning" is something I cherish. Many times, I have worked with students who felt that their future was bleak. Giving my students a glimmer of hope when working with them on difficult concepts was critical to their success and my own personal fulfillment. Teachers sacrifice so much daily for their students; it is imperative for educators to see the rays of sunshine in their work through all storm clouds they often face daily.

> For what it's worth: it's never too late or, in my case, too early to be whoever you want to be. There's no time limit, stop whenever you want. You can change or stay the same, there are no rules to this thing. We can make the best or the worst of it. I hope you make the best of it. And I hope you see things that startle you. I hope you feel things you never felt before. I hope you meet people with a different point of view. I hope you live a life you're proud of. If you find that

you're not, I hope you have the courage to start all over again. 99

~ *Francis Scott Fitzgerald*

The ability to appreciate the small things in life with a positive attitude is imperative to surviving major setbacks. Seeing things with gratitude elicits passion, joy, and purpose in our lives. When sharing appreciation with others, I have found we all can impact our social world in a positive way. My family members always demonstrate how to find joy in the little things in life, no matter what the season may bring us. During this past year, our family has a renewed appreciation for basic needs, family time, and the sacrifices of many who have worked tirelessly to help everyone negatively affected in 2020.

Finding the light in the little things is so important to my mother. She finds the positive in any situation and gives back to others. My mom shows appreciation to friends and family who helped in times of need. She volunteered by sewing masks and donating to agencies in need. She also cherishes the time she has now to sew quilts for cancer patients, volunteer with a variety of charities, and spend time with my father. My in-laws also cherish so many little things. My mother-in-law cherishes my father-in-law's smile, laughter, and sense of humor. We all are so grateful for living so close to one another. She is also grateful for the ability to sew, Texas sunrises and sunsets, and living close to her sons.

My husband is appreciative of little things that are so basic yet bring so much fulfillment and joy. He loves simplicity and the most direct path when solving any problems. We cherish peace and quiet in our home, and he loves to have down time with no distractions. He loves to take walks with our dogs, cooking, taking naps, and laughter.

I appreciate many things and am usually incredibly positive. However, many optimistic people break down during the issues we have faced this year. I have cried, sobbed, experienced a multitude of emotions. I cherish little things and acts of kindness. Little things help all of us to find the beauty of each day. It is truly the little things that keep us going and bring us happiness. For example, I rediscovered my love of learning while I worked with students from across the United States. I cherish my ability to support students in need during a pandemic, and to provide additional resources for their families.

I appreciate the time I was able to spend with my husband while we both worked at home during most of 2020. Plants have brought me joy as I started working in my yard. This small amount of gardening connected me with nature, created more optimism, and helped keep me grounded. I appreciated the time I could spend online through video conferencing. I loved being able to visit with family and still be able to connect. In addition, I am thankful for the opportunities that opened with all the changes of the year. I am thankful for counseling, yoga, and meditation to help me find my balance. I took a leap of faith and started my own tutoring company in 2020. Tutoring has rekindled my love of being a teacher and school counselor. I am learning so much through online classes and platforms. I am appreciative of all my experiences as an educator since these have shaped me to persist. There will be bumps, but I am excited to see what the next chapter has in store for me!

> ❝ We all have gifts and talents. When we cultivate those gifts and share them with the world, we create a sense of meaning and purpose in our lives. Squandering our gifts brings distress to our lives. As it turns out, it's not merely benign or "too bad" if we don't use the gifts that we've been given; we pay for it with our emotional and physical

well-being. When we don't use our talents to cultivate meaningful work, we struggle. We feel disconnected and weighed down by feelings of emptiness, frustration, resentment, shame, disappointment, fear, and even grief."

-*Brene Brown*

More About Kim:

Kim Peake, M.A., M.Ed., is a certified school counselor, school administrator, and teacher in Texas. As a passionate educator, Kim worked in public schools as a teacher and counselor before transitioning to virtual education and consulting. As a lifelong learner committed to personal growth, Kim has completed a bachelor and two master's degrees in the education field. Kim started her own Tutoring/Educational Consulting company, Reach Your Peake, LLC, in 2020. The company specializes in virtual tutoring, educational consulting, test preparation, and Social and Emotional Learning for students in Kindergarten-12th grade. She also works with students navigating the college & career process.

She published her first collaborative book with a group of women from Every Heart Project in 2017. Her story reveals her emotional journey of the first few years of her father's brain tumor diagnosis and treatment.

Kim volunteers for various charities and serves on multiple charity boards in North Texas. She loves to travel, spend time outdoors, socialize with friends, and watch hockey. Kim and her husband live in North Texas with their two spoiled fluffy Welsh Pembroke Corgis named Lizzie and Simon.

Contact Kim:

www.reachyourpeake.com
www.facebook.com/reachyourpeake

The Gift of Becoming

by Erica Figueroa

> For me, becoming isn't about arriving somewhere or achieving a certain aim. I see it instead as forward motion, a means of evolving, a way to reach continuously toward a better self.
>
> The journey doesn't end.
>
> ~ Michelle Obama

I woke up on May 10, 2020 and glanced at my phone; it was just after nine o'clock in the morning. I heard my husband and our girls stirring in the kitchen. It was Mother's Day. I rolled out of bed and washed up before making my way to see what they were doing.

I walked into the kitchen and saw sunlight coming in the kitchen windows. It was a beautiful day so full of possibilities. We said our "good mornings" and I kissed the girls. My husband, Jorge and my daughters had set a place for me at the table; they planned a cereal buffet for breakfast, which was rare! There were four different kinds to choose from. How fun was this? I chose Raisin Bran.

Right by my chair, there was a giant mylar balloon that looked like a humongous teacup and said, "World's Best Mom" on it. My daughter, Carmen, proudly presented me with a sweet card, which she had made herself. I gave her a warm hug, and then we bowed our heads to pray before digging into our cereal.

Jorge handed me a card, and I paused between bites of cereal to read it. I read the front of the card, and it said, *"God Will Take Care of You. For He has said, 'I will never leave you or forsake you.' Hebrews 13:5."* The card contained a sympathy-related narrative. Jorge also wrote a message inside, and it said, in part, *"I know this is a condolences card. LOL. It is a condolences card to you about the old you...I am so excited to see you through this. It's going to be fun, tough, hard, stressful, and totally worth it."* I read the card in its entirety, as tears threatened to spill over onto my cheeks. And then, they did.

To understand what happened this Mother's Day, we must go back several years to the summer of 2017. And honestly, it goes back even further than that; but that summer is when I started listening to my heart. It was not clear to anyone else. From outward appearances, I had my life together. I had been married almost ten years. We had two daughters, ages five and one. I was a working mom, secure and established in my career for fifteen years. We owned our home; we were blessed with the best family and friends. Everything was in order.

Everything was in order; yet, I felt like something was missing. Something was missing for a while. Something felt off, but I could not put my finger on it. I went to work every day in a public service position and still came home each night wondering if anything I did that day mattered. If I were to not show up one day, would anyone notice? I remember several times going to my parents' house after work and crying to my mom. There was a profound sadness I could not put into words; I was deeply emotional, and I did not know why. My mom would sit and hold my hand; her being there was such a comfort to me. She always listened and never judged. She never tried to tell me what to do or how to fix my problem, which I appreciated. She was so wise; she knew I needed to work through it on my own. I remember telling my husband I was bored. He was bewildered as he stared back at me. He did not understand me because he was on fire every day, excited to be working for himself in a business he loved. The guilt that came over me after these intense feelings of sadness was unreal. I was so blessed; how could I justify being sad when I had so much? It was not that I was ungrateful; believe me. I knew I was blessed to have family and friends. I knew I was blessed that my family had all we needed. My sadness told a different story. My sadness had me feeling there was something wrong with me for wanting more.

I reflected on my feelings. I realized I had closed myself off to new experiences, especially after having my second daughter, Celeste, I stopped setting new goals or trying to progress in any way. I gave everything to my family, and when it came to myself, I had nothing left. In general, I stopped making time for anything having to do with me. I put myself in a box and stopped growing as a person. In becoming a mom, I stopped making time for the things I loved before I even had children. I lost myself.

Subconsciously, I knew what I needed to do. I needed to open my mind and my heart not only to the old things I used to love but new things, too. I needed to learn new things. I needed to see progress made toward a goal. I needed to get excited again about new ideas and possibilities for my life. I needed to feel alive again. It was not until the following summer that I began to say, "yes" to things again after saying, "no" for so long. It really was like the movie <u>Yes, Man</u> with Jim Carrey. If you have not seen that movie, it is a good one!

I began to say "yes" to all kinds of things that normally would have easily been a "no."

I said, "yes" to losing twenty pounds.

I said, "yes" to meeting new people in networking groups.

I said, "yes" to running a barbecue catering side business.

I said, "yes" to learning more about blog writing and public speaking.

I said, "yes" to new goals like writing an essay for a collaborative book.

I said, "yes" to starting a dance-fitness-class side business of my own.

I said "yes" to feeding my mind with positive thoughts and ideas. I listened to podcast after podcast created by different people, hungry for the wisdom and different perspectives in each one.

I said "yes" to being more intentional about how I set my goals and how I set about doing my work and interacting with others.

I said "yes" to taking the wheel of my own life instead of sitting in the back seat as an observer to how my life was playing out. Something got into me, and I decided my world needed a little shaking up!

All these things I have said, "yes" to haven't necessarily been "my thing." But I have gained so much from each experience, either because I met new people, the experience taught me a lesson about life, or because the experience taught me more about myself.

What I am experiencing now and will not let go of for all the years I still have left in this world is that of trying on new things. I heard Christy Wright, author, and personality for Ramsey Solutions, compare it to trying on clothes. She said you sometimes see an outfit on the hanger, and you are not sure it's for you. You try it on, and it fits you like it was made for you. Other times you see something on the rack, and you think, *"this is just my style"* only to find it does not suit you. That's the way it is with things in this life. I've learned I can't stop learning or trying new things or progressing. The minute I stop advancing, I feel ineffective, and as if I've lost the purpose for my life.

That's a place to which I do not ever want to go back.

There was a Facebook post I recently read and re-posted on my Facebook page. The post was a story about a woman who asked God to put her back together because she was falling apart. God said it was okay for some of the pieces to fall away because she was shedding the things that no longer served her, and she was falling into place. She went on to say she was scared to change.

God told her she wasn't changing; she was becoming.

She asked who she was becoming. God responded, *"Becoming who I created you to be! A person of light and love, charity, hope, courage, joy, mercy, grace, and compassion. I made you for more than the shallow pieces you have decided to adorn yourself with that you cling to with such greed and fear. Let those things fall off you. I love you! Don't change! Become! Become! Become who I made you to be. I'm going to keep telling you this until you remember it."*

Then another piece fell off, and she asked if she was broken. God said she was not broken, but she was breaking like the dawn, and once more He told her to become. I found it to be so beautiful and moving.

The thing I let fall away from me were the limitations I put on myself. I replaced those limitations with an assurance that it's ok to want and strive for more. I express gratitude daily for the blessings in my life. I know now it's also ok to work for more and evolve into the best version of myself.

As I wiped my tears and continued to eat my cereal, I smiled. These were happy tears. These were tears of recognizing that difficult season for what it was and being happy as a new season began. The condolences card I received for Mother's Day wasn't typical, but nothing about the last couple of years was typical. It felt a little scary and a lot exciting. Through the process of trying new things, but also of letting go of old things that no longer served me, I was different. I was grateful for that difficult season because, without it, I would never have been able to appreciate where I was now.

I would never have appreciated the gift of becoming.

More About Erica:

By day, Erica Figueroa works in a leadership role in Public Service. She has worked in public service for 18 years and is most proud of the employee enrichment sessions she shares with staff members in her agency.

By night and on the weekends, she is a DivaDance® franchise owner. Dance has been a gift in Erica's life and now she loves to give the gift of dance away. She feels a sense of joy and affirmation that she's doing something worthwhile when a person takes a class and then goes out into the world perhaps a little nicer in their interactions with others because they feel good, are more confident, and healthier. She is married to her perfect match and is a mom to two sweet girls who inspire her to chase her dreams.

Contact Erica:

Instagram.com/intentionallyerica
Facebook.com/intentiondriven
Email: intentionallyerica@gmail.com

The Gift of Grief

by Christy Simpson

> *If you are so swallowed by grief in this moment that hope is nowhere to be found - I'll light a candle for your pain. The light will guide you home when you are ready.*
> ~ Cami Zea

When I began the outline for this chapter, I was approaching my 50th birthday and diving deep into all the self-examination that milestone brings. I had a completely different plan. The original chapter followed a highly sensitive person in our current society, showing empathy to those who may appear not to deserve it. In this version of the chapter, I overused the words toxic and narcissistic. Those labels of others have become trendy with today's self-help gurus but can do a complete disservice to our own growth and relationships.

Labeling allows us to write off anyone that may disagree with our values or even simply have the audacity to hold us accountable for our own actions when we are not strong enough for that level of feedback. We see it as being about them and their "issues," not as an opportunity to reflect on our own boundaries and authenticity – Have we communicated our expectations or boundaries to them, or are we just expecting them to know through magical mind-reading powers? Now, there absolutely are clinical narcissists and dangerously toxic people out there that do serious damage; abusive situations excluded, many of us have not actually encountered any. Every single person has moments where they are selfish, hurtful, and lacking in judgment, but if each of us were to be labeled as toxic or a narcissist every time we made a mistake that hurt someone, then where would we be? It is like we say at work: if everything is critical, then nothing is critical.

As a highly sensitive person making my way through life, there are a lot of people that cross my boundaries, disappoint me, or flat out hurt my feelings – even people that I love – but if I labeled everyone and dismissed them I would be very lonely.

As a matter of fact, I was labeled as a narcissist once. That person expected me to read their mind, and when I failed to do so and I disappointed them, they went on a "toxicity campaign." Their actions were painful, but they were not inherently bad or toxic. I understand now that they needed somewhere to focus their anger and sadness, and I was available as they waged their own internal war. My gift is a reminder to try and see the root of someone's actions before attempting to label them. Set new boundaries and make changes (even big hairy ones) if that is necessary to protect your own interests. If they really are clinical, then by all means seek help and get some distance.

I still feel like it is an important topic to examine, but as far as writing this chapter was concerned, life had a different plan…

Eleven days after that milestone birthday, I lost my big sister, Candy, to her battle with metastatic breast cancer resulting in acute liver failure. I was devastated. My world turned totally topsy turvy. Oh, it also happened right at the beginning of a global pandemic that would shut down society for two months and counting.

What would I write about now? Loss of a sibling and the "forgotten mourners" that lose both their past and future? Why we don't have a word like orphan or widow for people who lose siblings? Helping older parents deal with the loss of an adult child? Death in the midst of a pandemic and no ability to have services? Turning 50 and dealing with canceled celebrations? Prepping for a pandemic and the ensuing panic in suburbia? The gifts of sheltering in place? None of those felt like good gifts to share.

And then it hit me.

Grief.

When Candy left us, the grief hit me like a ton of bricks. It felt a lot like what I imagine the Wicked Witch of the East felt when Dorothy's house fell on her (BOOM!). In fact, now that I am writing this, I know why the Wicked Witch of the West was so witchy – she'd just lost her sister, too! But this time, perhaps grief was a gift from my sister to me. Sounds a little off, but stick with me – it's much like those elusive silver linings in a world of storms; sure, we'd all prefer not to have the storm in the first place (and just happily miss out on that silver lining), but life does not work like that. There will be storms, so we had better be able to discover the silver and gold in them. If we can't, then the storm may just swallow us up in its darkness.

Grief is not linear – it is winding, it is complex, and it is messy.

We are all familiar with the basic stages of grief – Denial/Isolation, Anger, Bargaining, Depression, and Acceptance. On paper, that sounds simple. It is like a checklist to work through. Endure each stage, and then we will feel better, things will go back to normal, and people will know how to interact with us again. Unfortunately, it doesn't work that way at all. What they forget to tell you is that at times you will feel nothing, and at other times you will feel everything at once. Everyone will experience grief in their own way. The stages of grief will not always hit us in order, and we can definitely expect to bounce between all of them multiple times.

One aspect of a terminal illness that is not discussed often is that those diagnosed with the illness, as well as their loved ones, must experience the grief process multiple times – not just when a loved one dies, but at the time of diagnosis and as the disease progresses – often while maintaining a normal life and without any external support (because they have not actually lost anyone yet). The process is the same, it is just a prolonged way of getting through it. It is as if someone were to stab you in the heart multiple times with a tiny needle and then sneak up on you with a huge butcher knife for that final blow.

At first, there is a sense of shock.

We walk in circles and do or say many things that we will not recall later.

This is *survival* mode.

Certainly, we have misunderstood what they told us – it is not really happening. They are just on a trip and will walk through the door at any moment. Someone has it WRONG! As I sped over to my sister's after getting the news, I shared with a friend that she had died. I briefly had a thought about how many people I would have to call and apologize to for sharing incorrect news in the event that I got there and they were wrong (they were not wrong). Later, I got mad. I was mad at her, I was mad at her doctors, I was mad at people for not calling me, I was mad at people FOR calling me, I was mad at people for talking (and also for not talking), I was mad at the wind for blowing. I was *so incredibly angry*. But I was not really angry with all those people – it was just a projection of my grief. It is sometimes easier to be mad at random people and the people we love the most than to look the loss in the face and see it for the monster that it is. It mocks our grief and relishes in our pain.

Anger I can deal with. It is familiar. Anger and I are old friends. But the next stage of grief is the most gut-wrenching.

The questions that rip out your heart:

If I had known that dinner was the last time I would see her alive, would I have done anything different?

If I had noticed (enter anything here) sooner, could I have gotten her the help that she needed?

If I had insisted that she do x or y, would I have gotten another day with her?

What action could I have taken, or thing could I have done to save my sister from dying?

Our minds are powerful, and sometimes quite cruel. Logically, we know that we are not all-powerful and magical, but we become convinced that WE could have stopped our loved one's death in its tracks. This is a stage in which it is easy to get stuck. The guilt almost feels "right." It feels bad and awful, just like we think we should feel. But to get lost in the guilt is not healthy; it is not fair to our heart, and it is not fair to those that are still with us and love us. It is also one of the stages that will come back and surprise you with multiple rounds.

Good times.

As we work through those violent and messy emotions, another stage permeates everything – the sadness and depression. This part is so unique to everyone, but it is big, and it is hairy. It can be anything from worrying about the services and if they are appropriate to honor those lost, to all the people and things that we missed supporting while we were stuck in our process. Some days basic self-care – like bathing or brushing our teeth – feels insurmountable, so we curl up on our bed and sob, sometimes for days.

Sometimes we keep going through daily life looking like nothing is wrong, but inside there is a cavern so deep it feels like the universe itself would not fill it.

This is normal.

ALL of it.

Only once it becomes an issue for our safety (or the safety of others, especially dependents) do we really need to examine our patterns. Whether an issue or not, getting some outside and/or professional support will usually help! It is hard to ask for the hugs and support we might need at this time. If we are lucky, we have people that can read through our walls and safety barriers to be there when we need them. They are the ones that persist and remember to send a batch of cookies or a thoughtful message long after the original wave has passed. Often, we must do a little more of the reaching out to make sure we get the support and gentle comforts that we need. Either way, we survive each wave that makes it our way. Somehow, they either get a little easier, or we become more skilled surfers.

Eventually, in the midst of all the dark feelings of anger, sorrow, guilt, and confusion, one tiny ray of acceptance shines through. We are not through the raging storm at all, but there is a brief glimmer of hope. Typically, it is fleeting, like a whiff of gardenia on a breeze, but it is tangible, and we try to grab hold. It is in those moments that we receive one of the gifts of grief, introspection. The fog lifts and we begin to think a little more clearly. Oh, our stormy friends have not left us – they simply allow us moments of clarity where we recall the fun things. Memories do not always take us to a dark place, and we start to dive deep into our beliefs. Comfort lives here. It is here that the higher power or universe that you believe in starts to show you the signs. Signs of your loved one's presence and spirit.

Regardless of what you believe, lean into it. Look for the answers to questions we have long held. As our fog lifts, before we get pulled back into the minutiae of life, are some of the clearest, defining moments we can have on Earth, while our soul is stripped and bare. We can take this opportunity to prioritize the things that really matter now. Our perception has been adjusted and we know what it can mean to take something so very precious to us for granted and then watch it get ripped away from us. One caution though: we have to make certain it is not a grief reaction that we are labeling as clarity or a means to fill that cavernous hole that remains – many grand mistakes have been made there in the name of progress and growth. We must make sure it is at a moment when we have been able to work through some of the emotions and we can find genuine moments to smile amongst the tears.

I still have a lot of work to do and many emotions to process, but I feel like I can accept and trust in the process now, instead of railing against it at every turn or hiccup. As much as I would prefer to have my beautiful sister back here beside me, I am thankful for her gifts of love, memories, grief, and perspective. I hope as you progress through life and experience loss, when the time is right, that you can start to see the gifts provided by the one you so dearly miss.

Big love to all your hearts!

More About Christy:

Christy Simpson has worked in the telecom industry at a top ten Fortune 500 company for over 20 years, gaining specialized knowledge in organizational IT program management, client relationships, and complex puzzle resolution. As a seasoned program manager, she is passionate about predicting client needs and offering unique solutions. In addition to being a US patent holder, she is the founder and owner of Positively CFRS and SeaSquared Travel, where she helps others curate a balanced and happy life. Outside of the office, Christy enjoys luxury travel, her family (especially her husband and two dogs), painting, and spending time with friends.

Contact Christy:

Website: www.positivelycfrs.com
Facebook.com/positivelycfrs
Instagram.com/positivelycfrs

The Gift of Growth

by Jodie West

Strength and growth come only through continuous effort and struggle.

~ Napoleon Hill

As I have walked, and sometimes even ran, through each chapter of my life thus far, I choose to reflect upon my choices and actions and constantly ask myself if I am being true to myself and living authentically and with integrity. Although I strive to exude positivity and resolve, my commitment is to serve God through faith, family, friends, and my work. Every single person I interact with should be a reflection of those values and beliefs.

I admit many of my past relationships have not been beneficial or healthy. I've had to find the courage and strength to walk away from those who sought to distract me, dishonor me, or discourage me from being my authentic self. I tend to see the good in everyone, often missing the blatant red flags that others might see with ease. Perhaps realizing why I am often drawn into these relationships is the lesson I've had to learn, which I always pair with my faith in God that the lessons are, in fact, teaching me what I need to know to learn and grow.

My first serious romantic relationship was with a gentleman I met while developing my leadership skills as an assistant manager at McDonald's. Throughout our relationship, he formed and molded me into the fiancé he envisioned to be his soulmate and true love, all the while criticizing my style and image. One day I looked in the mirror and I no longer saw myself looking back at me. I saw his perfect wife, or what he had described, but the real me was gone. It was then I realized our relationship was really an illusion of what others thought we were, but not actually a healthy relationship. It was built on a shaky foundation, ultimately crumbling under pressure. My mother was especially surprised when I cancelled the future wedding plans, but I know I dodged a bullet with that decision.

For my next relationship, for some crazy reason, I turned to a former high school classmate who had been asking about me through my mother. Rebound is definitely a good word to describe it, but I liked who I was in the mirror because it finally felt more like me. I was growing into an independent, authentic, goal-oriented and ambitious woman! I probably treated him like more of a doormat at times, even though he tried his best, but looking back I should have known the challenges of a rebound relationship. When we found out a child was on the way, we did the expected thing to do, which was get married. It didn't last very long, though, and I coupled the decision to end it with an escape to my next adventure in Texas, my precious son in tow.

A year later I was thriving in my new leadership position and I felt the ambitious drive within me when an unexpected gift arrived: an absolutely amazing adventurous relationship! Unfortunately, my newfound freedom and joy catapulted me right into a true con man who possessed no integrity, but we sure did have some adventures for a couple of years! This relationship was ultimately devastating, though it taught me a lot about both myself and my son. We are resilient, strong, and we can rebuild when we turn back to faith in God. We also learned strong lessons about the value of family and being true to ourselves, no matter what.

A few years later I was introduced to my next husband, a man I felt needed my guidance, so he became my next project. I naively thought I could fix him, lead him, and share what I had learned about authenticity. I later realized I was simply searching for stability, which I didn't find in that relationship. I had zero faith that I deserved a good, healthy relationship, which ended up proving true. Despite truly thriving in my leadership role at work, it seemed as though the red flags on the home front were flying higher and brighter, but I still couldn't see it. My family was afraid to speak up and try to intervene, and looking back, I understand now. I had spent so many years with controlling, manipulative men, and now I was in another toxic relationship and trying to fix someone who refused to help themselves. After several suicide attempts during our marriage, I finally walked away. He ultimately died by suicide a year after our divorce was final.

I have no regrets.

All of these relationships truly helped shape me into the authentic and powerful woman I've become today. I am thankful for those with whom I have crossed paths, and even the darkest of days taught me incredible and humbling lessons. In my life and in my career, I strive to provide guidance and advice to others to help them achieve their biggest dreams and goals, no matter how big or small.

Finally, I am excited to share that I finally found the love of my life, even though I wasn't looking for him. I ended up creating a profile on an internet dating website called Match, and I was pleasantly surprised when I met him for the first time. Just over 13 years ago, we met up at a local wine bar, where I ordered a flight of red wines. He spent most of the evening begging me to share all about my scuba diving stories. It was a fabulous evening that ended with a quick goodnight kiss and hope for another date.

He's been with me ever since, and these two self-reliant and authentic Aquarians pair perfectly. He stood by my side when I lost my mother, who was also his biggest fan and loved when he sang her Elvis songs. I truly believe she fell in love with him while I was still figuring it out. He supported me through various employment changes and pivots, including a deceptive work partnership that had to be dissolved. And most recently, he held my hand as I mourned the loss of my father, the most authentic man I'd ever known.

I'm humbled to share I finally found my soulmate, and I'm thankful for the winding road that led me to him. I wouldn't change a thing.

Through all of this, my career path as a Financial Advisor allows me to share guidance and education while developing long-lasting relationships with my clients.

It is never too early or too late to start planning for the future.

More About Jodie:

Jodie has been in the financial services industry for over twenty years working with both business owners and high net-worth individuals in creating, preserving and transferring their wealth. Jodie uses her knowledge and expertise to assist clients through their journey in creating their financial strategies to improve their potential to accomplish their financial goals.

Jodie has a background in Accounting with an emphasis in Economics. Jodie's licenses include life, health, disability income and long-term care insurance as well as her general lines property and casualty licenses in Texas. She also holds a FINRA Series 7 Registration for General Securities and Series 66. She has earned the Certification in Long Term Care (CLTC) designation. Jodie is on the Leadership team for Women Helping Women 2 Network and an active member of Every Heart Project.

Jodie married her soul mate, Dave and currently enjoys sharing their home in Sachse and spending time with their children and grandsons. They enjoy kayaking, horseback riding, scuba diving, reading, and traveling. She also enjoys exploring her creative side in her custom Jewelry and Gift business. Jodie is from Iowa and transferred to Texas in late 1984 to raise her son and pursue her career.

Contact Jodie:

Email: Jodie@stonewaterplanning.com

The Gift of Happiness

by Catherine Paour

> *You can't connect the dots looking forward; you can only connect them looking backwards. So you have to trust that the dots will somehow connect in your future.*
> ~ Steve Jobs

Back in the 1960s, when I was 9 years old, I got my first pair of eyeglasses. They were tiny blue plastic cat-eye frames. Suddenly everything looked vivid and clear and I could read the school chalkboard for the first time. I guess I never knew what I was missing but it sure seemed like a miracle! It was then that I learned my gift of listening to my gut when it pertained to my own body. I have spent the last five decades unraveling all the layers until once again, and again and again, I was finally able to connect the dots to learn exactly what was wrong and gain the clarity I needed most.

I was born double breech, or as I like to put it laughingly, butt first! I guess they did not turn babies back in 1960. It was highly likely they did not even know my position until my butt surprised the doctor, following by my feet getting stuck! My mom describes seeing both of my legs crossed over my left shoulder and my left arm tangled underneath them. My two older brothers had to hold my legs down so my mom could change me, and I had to wear 3 to 4 cloth diapers to keep my legs from springing back up like rubber bands. I did not walk until I was two years old. In grade school, I was miserable in physical education and wheezed all the time. I cried whenever I had to run or jump, though I never knew why.

I always felt like I just could not catch my breath. I had no idea it was not normal, just like seeing a fuzzy world before finally getting glasses at age 9. Following several trips to the emergency room at the early age of 12, I was diagnosed with asthma and a heart murmur. My high school years were spent passing out after my morning shower and hiding it from my mom, as well as suffering the humiliation of being placed in adaptive physical education due to my limitations. Near the end of my junior year, I had the pleasure of wearing a full body cast in an attempt to correct my Scoliosis. I remember lying down in the back seat of our station wagon to travel places, and I had to lean against the corner of a classroom because I couldn't sit down in a desk chair. I had to wear maternity pants over the cast, and it felt like it had concrete-like fake boobs. I was no expert, but I assumed that wasn't the ideal way to get my high school crush to notice me!

I have worked full-time since the age of 16, and at 23 got a job at a local medical center as a receptionist in Human Resources. Unfortunately, I failed the new hire physical and was told they required cardiac clearance before they could give me a firm start date. Though I was scared, I booked an appointment with my grandfather's cardiologist. He certainly heard the heart murmur but ultimately cleared me for employment. My parents were in Hawaii at the time, and I was afraid to tell them until they got home.

I got married in 1997 and two months later had a Trans Ischemic Attack (TIA), also known as a mini stroke. I saw my cardiologist and a neurologist and had complete workups. In 1999 I was pregnant and miserable, beyond what appeared to be standard among my friends. Delivery was brutal, and I honestly thought my body wouldn't survive it. After working at the medical center for 19 years, I left for a new job and a fresh start with my own little family.

I continued to see my cardiologist every three to six months since I was always having issues, and eventually moved to a new doctor who was well respected in the medical center where I worked. I always complained to him that I couldn't carry my growing baby or get groceries from my car to the kitchen without feeling weak or out of breath. Frustrated and seeking answers, I sought out at least half a dozen other specialists. I was called a hypochondriac, and one even wrote, "very sick" in my chart. My doctor diagnosed me with Congestive Heart Failure at the age of 42 but had no explanation as to why. Being a mom of a toddler, I was terrified, but at least I finally had an answer and learned how to manage my condition. As time went on, I became worse. I experienced shortness of breath and debilitating edema that caused my legs to feel like concrete pillars. I suffered from horrible digestion, scary heart palpitations, visual disturbances, and I passed out a lot. Still, I powered through it all to keep my job. My heart rate would soar in an instant to nearly 200 beats per minute and last for hours, and I would often lose my faculties during an episode. Imagine feeling like you just ran a marathon for the first time, and you never even moved!

One day, in fact the same day I was laid off my job, my husband walked out on me. It was disappointing but caring for my baby and myself was my highest priority, so I viewed this as a blessing.

A couple of years later, I underwent 3 Cardiac Ablations, a surgical procedure where they enter the heart through a catheter and cauterize, or burn, the areas in the heart that are misfiring. I also had 3 Cardioversions, which are chemically induced restarts of the heart. It seemed like my parents were always in Hawaii when these things happened! I felt like such a regular at the emergency room and dreaded going through my extensive medical history with each physician. And every doctor, nurse, and technician said the same thing: "You're so young to have all this going on." My cardiologist wasn't able to explain the cause of my heart failure, and the numerous pulmonologists I saw were dumbfounded by my severely reduced lung capacity of 52%, which was first measured at the age of 17.

I thanked God every day for the Handicap Accessible Parking placard I eventually got! When my son was 7 years old, I bought a used electric scooter to take him to places like Disneyland and the Zoo. I dreaded going anywhere that had walking, stairs, or no seating. I had excluded myself from anything physical for the last 15 years, which also meant losing friends and fun opportunities. And forget about trying to date!

Finally, after another decade of constant physical ailments, stress, and strain, I begged my cardiologist of the last 30 years to dig deeper. I pleaded with him, saying, *"I simply can't breathe."* It was apparent to me I had insulted him, but I just knew there was something else we could do. I demanded answers. I had annual echocardiograms, swallowed handfuls of heart medications daily, and even fashioned my own oxygen tank I had to carry around with me, showing off tubes up my nose. I insisted on every diagnostic test imaginable, and still nothing. I never felt sorry for myself, but I felt sorry for my young son who had to watch his mom go through so much medical mayhem.

When my son was 15 years old, I was a decade into an exhausting corporate job, I decided to work with a Life Coach to reignite my sparkle! I had so many dreams, passions, and projects I wanted to do but never had the energy. She helped me peel back the layers and asked me one pivotal question, *"What gets in the way of you pursuing your dreams?"* I told her it was my lack of energy and stamina. It was exhausting being a single mom, working full-time, and struggling with my health. Truth be told, all I wanted to do was go home after work and collapse into the bed. She helped me make a commitment to myself to implement self-care strategies. She also suggested I step out of my comfort zone and seek out a new cardiologist after 30 years. Though I dreaded having to explain my five decades of medical history to a new doctor, I did it! Within a week and after just one test in the Cardiac Cath Lab, my new kind (and young) cardiologist came into my recovery room, and she hesitantly asked me, *"Has anyone ever told you that you have a hole in your heart?"* My mom and I were both shocked, and I answered, *"uh....noooooo,"* in a strange tone.

She drew a picture showing how my good oxygenated blood was colliding with the unoxygenated blood, and, well, no wonder I felt like crap! She went on to explain that it was called an Atrial Septal Defect. It is a congenital heart defect I was born with and have lived with my entire life, undiagnosed for 55 years! I was almost happy to hear this, but my mind kept questioning, *"how could a cardiologist of 30 years not have told me that?"* She, too, was quite shocked. A couple of angiograms were needed to see how much damage there was to the heart and if I was a candidate for open heart surgery to repair it. The hole was large, and I soon learned that not just any thoracic surgeon could do this. It was quite stressful to have surgery so far away from home, but I was truly looking forward to my "new normal" and energy for life, with lots of good oxygen, stamina, and wellness to fully become a woman of purpose and passion! I was excited at the thought of re-imagining my future, which I thought could actually include walking, talking, laughing, and breathing all at the same time! As I reflected on all my years of declining health, I kept thinking to myself, *"it would have been really helpful to know that my heart had a giant hole."*

Every medical professional I came in contact with after that raised their eyebrows and exhibited shocked facial expressions upon learning this went undiagnosed for so long. "How could he (the cardiologist) have missed it?" was something I was asked over and over again. The surgeon described the hole as "enormous," and I had an atrial aneurysm. Most holes in the heart are measured in millimeters and can be closed with a mesh plug through a catheter, but mine measured 6 x 3 centimeters! He said the septal wall was "basically non-existent," and my heart was just one great big "swamp." I was told I was lucky to be alive. He was able to reconstruct my heart and build a septal wall using my heart pericardium. I was never afraid and managed to find the humor in every step of the journey. More than anything, I was looking forward to going from feeling crappy to happy.

The surgery went well, and I made a point to have fun every step of the way. I remember having to sterilize myself and walk to the hospital from a nearby hotel at 5 o'clock in the morning! I made my parents take pictures of me on life support. And once it was removed, I had everyone laughing. I really wanted to put makeup on, and I hate to go without my lipstick. Perhaps I was trying to flirt? But then my surgeon told me my skin tone was different from when I arrived at the hospital.

I did not understand until I finally looked at myself in a mirror. I was so surprised; my skin was beautiful! It is funny what "good" oxygen will do for you!

After 5 days, I was discharged from the hospital and could not wait to get home. My then 80-year-old mom spent the entire day prepping food and cleaning up after my teenage son, who had been home alone. Thankfully, he was able to drive, and it was comforting to know that he could run errands, take me to appointments and help me during my recovery. After a long day, my mom finally went home both worried and exhausted. My son took the dogs out for a walk, dropped them off back home, then left for his 3-mile run he did every night. I remember saying to myself, *"ahhh, it's finally quiet!"*

Little did I know that my son clipped a corner on his run, fell, and was lying on someone's front yard, unable to get up! He did not want to alarm me, so he called my parents and asked them to find him and pick him up. At the time, I had no idea of any of this. My exhausted parents were driving around my neighborhood and apparently couldn't find him. Meanwhile, my son called me and told me what happened, and that *"Gramma and Grampa keep driving right past me!"* I told him to turn on his iPhone flashlight and wave it around. Thankfully, they finally found him. My mom dropped my dad off at my house and took my son to the emergency room. My 85 year-old dad, who we lovingly call "Gramps," was roaming around my kitchen looking for a treat and said he could not understand how anyone could have a house without cookies! I guess he couldn't understand why I had not been to the store. Around midnight, my mom brought my son home with a broken foot and a sprained ankle. And it was his right foot, of course, which meant he could no longer take himself to and from school, help me get up and around the house, or run errands to the store. So, there we were, both pretty much worthless!

I felt so overwhelmed and incapable of anything. As the days dragged on, I sounded like a beached walrus trying to get out of bed. I was loaded with tape all around my jugular and neck down to my stomach. I had a device attached to my sternum I had to lug around with me 24/7 that provided suction to my chest incision with a power pack purse. Both of my arms were completely black from so many needle sticks at the hospital, my breathing was shallow, and my neck was killing me. My two little Yorkies could not understand why they could not jump on me in bed. My house could have used a good scrub down, and I was fairly sure I needed a scrub down as well. My pillows sucked, my doorbell didn't work for my visitors, and I was dying for an adjustment with my chiropractor. On top of it all, we were in the midst of a vicious heatwave, and I couldn't open the freezer door to get ice (too much suction). I did not have much of an appetite, but I kept thinking, "good - this better help me lose weight!" Thank God for automatic bill-pay, remote controls, and my iPhone.

Just 3 weeks later, my parents left on a 15-day Hawaiian cruise they had booked the year before. They were incredibly worried about leaving me, but I was feeling better and assured them I would be okay. Who would have guessed that 5 days later I would end up back at the hospital with heart failure, tachycardia, oxygen desaturation, A-fib, blood clots, pulmonary edema, and a host of other complications? That turned into a week in the ICU, and there was even mention of a possible heart transplant! I continued to find humor in everything, like when I was wrapped in a blanket while sitting on a commode in the ICU when two friends came to see me - just as a handsome, hunky doctor also arrived to check on me. My friends sat there admiring the dreamy doctor with mouths wide open and fanning themselves, as I sat there secretly peeing and trying to keep a straight face! I also knew that there was no way I wanted my parents to find out about this while on their amazing Hawaiian cruise.

I never posted anything on social media because I was afraid my dad would find it on Facebook at their next port of call! I knew my mom was going to check in with me when they arrived in Maui, and I had better be prepared with what I planned to say. She attempted to call my cell phone 4 days into my hospital stay, just as I was being assisted to the hospital bathroom. I then made sure there were no medical personnel, rings, buzzes, or alarms in my hospital room when I returned her call. I tried not to cry as I told my mom everything was great and not to worry! She had no clue where I was or that I was not able to drive my son to school every day since he broke his foot. I totally lied and felt awful about it. I hung up just in time as a nurse brought me a rinse-free shampoo cap for my hair. As I was massaging the cap into my scalp, eyes closed, it felt so amazing and refreshing. Suddenly, I remembered those commercials where the woman is washing her hair and moaning almost in ecstasy, and I could definitely relate. I probably made a few noises as I enjoyed the moment. Then I sensed a presence in my room, and I opened my eyes to find a tour of nursing students standing in my doorway. I cracked up laughing and said, *"Oh...hello!"*

I was discharged after a week, but still had a lot of recovery time ahead of me. A week after that, I picked my parents up from the Port of Los Angeles and heard all about their cruise. Then I confessed to them, telling them everything I had endured. Weeks later, I was not breathing well. I ended up back on oxygen for a while and my recovery kept having setbacks. Things got even worse a few months later when I began Cardiac Rehab and broke my tailbone on an exercise machine. I was back to lying down in the backseat of a car just like 40 years earlier when I wore my body cast!

It is so important to be filled with hope, happiness, and humor when dealing with health challenges and your healing journey. My career as a patient is perpetual, having been through 13 surgeries and more recently diagnosed severe sleep apnea, severely deviated septum, restrictive lung defect, digestive disorder, and hypothyroidism, to name a few. Throw in 2 additional surgeries and a broken leg last month! Hmm…. I wonder if I am ready to date yet!

My son is now 21 years old and serves in the US Navy as a Medic. My parents are celebrating their 65th anniversary and dream of going to Hawaii for the 49th time, but we are right smack in the crisis of a global pandemic. I am now in self-isolation, and always focusing on my health and happiness. People say I look great, and I laugh to myself and think, *"I'm defective, not dilapidated!"* Not all sick people look crappy, and some of us are really happy! And I will never stop connecting the dots, as it has also led me to discover my purpose and passions.

Every heart has a story, every heart has a purpose, every heart has a voice, and every heart has a gift.

But not every heart has a hole, and my hole heart and I have never been happier.

More About Catherine:

As a young girl, Catherine was envious of kids who could run, and she always felt left behind. As a young adult, she thrived in leadership and community service, rather than engaging in physical activities. As a grown woman, she became more aware of her intuition and finally realized she had it all along. Every surgery she had, plus the birth of her baby put her at extreme risk for survival because of what she did not know. Today, she often reflects and thinks to herself, *"it would have been really helpful to know, that my heart had a giant hole."*

Catherine shares her stories of health challenges and offers tips from her experience as a perpetual patient. Her courage to share her missed diagnoses with hope, happiness, and humor is both interesting and inspiring. She also advocates for trusting your intuition and learning how to manage your own healthcare needs and medical records, contrary to our "managed care" system.

Catherine is also dedicated to presenting the facts to medical and legal experts to raise awareness of the gaps in the gold standard of care, and how these fallacies can have a direct impact on the survival of a patient.

Catherine was born and raised in Torrance, California and her family has over a century of history of all being born in the same hospital and graduating from the same high school. She has one son, serving as a medic in the US Navy and is enjoying her retirement cuddling with her new rescue dog, playing the Ukulele, and supporting women by sharing her leadership and creative gifts with Christian writers and small businesses.

Catherine is also a contributing author in "Crappy to Happy: Sacred Stories of Transformational Joy" releasing October 2020 by Sacred Stories Publishing.

Contact Catherine:

Website: www.holeheartedcourage.com
Email: holeheartedcourage@gmail.com
Phone: 310-346-6096

The Gift of Leadership

by Gina Doerr

> *Before you are a leader, success is all about growing yourself. When you become a leader, success is all about growing others.*
>
> ~ *Jack Welch*

I sat quietly in the car, looking out the window at the miles of red, flat dirt of West Texas passing by, missing my friends in Pennsylvania, and wondering how I was going to go through all of this again, making new friends in a new place. This was move number...I don't know, maybe five or six, not counting moves within the same state. This one seemed to be the hardest out of all of them. I had been in Eastern Pennsylvania for almost four years (living in a few different towns), and this was my first move after starting high school. I lived in a small town named Carbondale, just outside of Scranton. I had a group of friends I adored, and I had built roots in the community. I volunteered at the local hospital near my house, had my favorite book

74

and coffee shop I visited almost daily, and could easily walk to any of my friends' houses to hang out. I was happy there, and it felt like home. Interestingly, I did feel a sense that I was meant for bigger things than what that town provided. Even at the age of fourteen, I knew I would most likely move away for school if things didn't change before then. And when I was fifteen, everything changed again.

My family and I were moving from Pennsylvania to Amarillo, Texas, and as we got closer to our destination, I truly began to believe I was on Mars. Miles of red clay stretched out before me, big, blue skies that seemed to go on forever, and until we reached bigger cities, it seemed like the homes were so far apart from their neighbors. I had never seen anything like it before, even having lived outside of Dallas about five years before this. It was very intimidating and created a sense of anxiety along with my grief over losing my friends. What I didn't know then was how this move, and all the others before and after, would set the stage for my growth as a person and a leader.

Growing up, I moved quite a bit. First, because my father was in the Navy when I was very young. And later, starting around six years old, several years after my parents divorced, I moved a lot because my stepfather was very ambitious and constantly on the lookout for the 'bigger, better' job. My mom was supportive of his career and that set the tone for our lives going forward. I was born in Virginia, and also lived in Maryland, New Jersey, Texas, and Pennsylvania. I was in both Maryland and Texas more than once. I attended several different schools in elementary school, middle school, and even high school. My fifth grade year alone was in three different schools between New Jersey, Maryland, and Texas. I took it for granted that this was my life, but now it occurs to me that chronicling my life could make for an interesting tale.

Fast forward one more move after Amarillo, and I found myself back in the Dallas area. I was there for a few years with my family and had just started college when my family decided to move again to Austin. In this case, the move was necessary as my stepdad was laid off and the job market was challenging for him. I was two years into college at the time, was working full-time for the YMCA, and in a serious relationship with my (now) husband. I had several discussions with my parents about staying in Dallas, and thankfully they respected my wishes and helped me stay there to finish school.

One of the best things to happen to me was getting a job at the YMCA right after I graduated high school. I had been struggling with finding the right job and my mom suggested getting into aquatics as a lifeguard for the summer and as a college job. She helped me get into a training class, which was the start of my enduring love for the YMCA, what it stands for, and the experiences it ultimately brought to my life. This was my first real opportunity to shine as a leader and I soaked up everything I could. I started as a lifeguard and quickly became a swim instructor. From there I became a trainer of lifeguards, trained in CPR/ First Aid, trained others to be swim instructors, became a supervisor, and led emergency response efforts at my local branch. I taught every age group from babies at six months old to adults in their seventies. I was doing something I loved and giving back to the community, which fed my passion and my caregiver soul. Another valuable experience which imparted several lessons upon my life was working with the Special Olympics swim team and teaching private lessons called Adapted Aquatics. I worked with individuals with Down Syndrome, cerebral palsy, dwarfism, and those all along the autism spectrum. Those students taught me patience, joy, pride in achievements, and what it means to be strong in the midst of adversity. I can never be thankful enough for the seventeen years I spent serving through the YMCA.

I believe my 'giver' mentality and my experience with the YMCA led me to pursue a job in the Human Resource field. I wanted a career where I could actively work with people in different functional areas and provide opportunities for training and development. I graduated with my HR degree in 2005 and fortuitously got my first HR job through someone I met at the YMCA. I met her through a healthy challenge program, and as chance would have it, she was looking for an HR admin role and I was looking for a way to break into my career field.

This fateful meeting led me to my now fourteen-year long career as a Human Resource professional. I have had the opportunity to grow as a person and in my career due to the amazing companies I have worked for and the leaders who helped me along my way. I have been able to fulfill my passion for training and development and see the change in others to realize their dreams. That is the biggest payoff for me. I have made mistakes along the way that have taught me to be confident and strong yet caring and understanding. One situation I remember is a former manager telling me that I needed to be cool and professional and keep a certain distance from others. While I understood what they were trying to teach, I politely disagreed. It is possible to maintain professional distance while still being kind and caring. I had to learn that the hard way, and I am thankful for those lessons. I am the person and professional I want to be, and it has provided me success in my career. We all have to find our own paths and realize how our dreams will work for us. All these experiences have instilled in me the confidence to lead, support, and show others the path to their own potential. I believe with all my heart we have the strength to accomplish our dreams and desires. I have endless faith in others' ability to change, grow and realize their gifts. I have seen it happen time after time, and I have seen it in myself. One of my life goals is to share that confidence and hope with others so that they, too, can become their best selves.

As I look back upon all those years of changing schools, changing towns, and changing states, I realize it taught me valuable lessons that are still with me today. I learned how to make friends with different people, even people in different regions of the United States. I learned how to maintain my academic excellence no matter what school I attended. I had to adapt and be flexible to my changing circumstances to be successful. All these qualities shaped me as a person and a leader and enabled me to take initiative where others might feel fear or insecurity. Also, I understand that what we worry about on the other side of our dreams is not as difficult as we think it is. At the time of all the changes in my life, I would sometimes feel sad for what I lost or feel sorry for myself. In retrospect, I had a great childhood that gave me the tools I needed to be my most authentic self. I learned to be strong, to hold my head high, and to share those gifts with others that hadn't found their voices yet. For that, I will always be grateful.

More About Gina:

I am a Human Resources professional with 14 years of experience in the HR field with a passion for training and development. I have eliminated waste in the areas of Human Resources and safety by focusing on process efficiencies. I have a history of commitment to employee engagement and strategic initiatives to drive talent management and the sustainability of successes. My goal is to provide the best customer service to both the employer and employee by demonstrating strong, consistent leadership and by creating an enriching work environment for all.

Contact Gina on LinkedIn: http://linkedin.com/in/gina-doerr-sphr-a7655215

The Gift of Healing

by Melody Self

> ❝ For I know the plans I have for you," declares the Lord,
> "Plans to prosper you and not to harm you, to give you
> hope and a future. ❞
>
> ~ Jeremiah 29:11

"This isn't the Christmas you want. It's the Christmas you are getting. Your son has stage 4 cancer."

I was in a shock. What did she say? What did the doctor mean that my son has cancer? Daniel was only 17 years old. Christmas Eve was only two days away, and the house was busy preparing for the holiday. Apparently, I had missed a call the night before from the doctor's office, and they called again early that morning. They instructed me to come immediately. I was paralyzed for a moment. We needed to eat breakfast. We needed to make arrangements for the other 6 kids in the house. This was too much. Then the doctor's office advised they had the Oncologist on the phone, and they wanted to admit my son to the hospital today. The hospital began calling shortly after, trying to coordinate our arrival. We lived two hours away and were still trying to figure out how to do this. I wasn't ready for my son to have surgery. I wasn't ready for my son to have cancer. Oh, and it's still almost Christmas. This isn't what I imagined for my Christmas. I told my 4 year-old daughter I'd be back soon to finish wrapping gifts with her.

How could this happen to me? I was one of the most holistic people I knew. How could I have a son with cancer? I was a certified natural health professional. I didn't feed my kids sugar, gluten, or dairy, even though people always told me I was too strict. I had a son who was allergic to sugar, and consuming it meant he would end up in the emergency room. So instead I fed them green smoothies and lots of veggies. I made alternatives to everything. I took pride in teaching people how to live an alkaline lifestyle. In fact, I was eating vegan at the time.

It felt like a nightmare, much like the nightmares I remember having as a kid. I would wake up terrified if the night light had burned out. I hugged my oversized stuffed bunny rabbit tightly, as if my life might depend upon him having to rescue me with his long legs and arms. He was taller than me, and that brought me comfort, yet I cried and cried because I knew a monster might still find me. The terror I felt left me wide awake in the dark, unable to move, paralyzed in fear. I had a room all to myself, so no one ever heard me. No one ever consoled me. No one ever came to my aid. I was all alone in my terror. My two younger sisters slept in another room. Sometimes I would wake feeling like I was being choked, gasping for air. I would be screaming for help, but no sound would come. I cried inwardly, silently. Sometimes I imagined

I was floating, and I could fly. It felt like I wasn't in my body and I was safe from any monster that was trying to hurt me or attack me.

I was finally on the road to the children's hospital with my son and his younger brother, Grayson, who had come to support. We drove the two hours to the hospital. I was praying silently the whole time, talking to God. When we arrived in the parking lot, I received another call from the doctor asking where I was. (I guess they were upset I didn't get there sooner.) It was strange how we were greeted like we were famous. Nurses, doctors, interns, medical staff filled the room, performing test after test all night long. It seemed to be never-ending and there was no one for me to talk to or lean on. There was no chaplain or advocate. They had all gone home to celebrate their Christmas with their families. I was left alone to navigate my emotions. I just kept praying and talking to God. I asked for wisdom. I reached out to a few people, but it was hard knowing who I could trust.

My son thought the doctor was lying to him. In fact, he was angry with me for taking him to the doctor. He asked me, *"Why are they saying this to me?"* He was non-responsive when they asked him questions. It was suspected that Daniel had cancer in his blood. He needed a blood transfusion overnight so that he would be ready for surgery in the morning. I felt like such a bad mom. How could I not know he was so sick? I had taken him in to get checked out three months earlier. They told me he had a muscle spasm in his neck, and I treated him for that. He even said that his younger brother, Eli, had hurt his neck in a football game they were playing. I remember asking the doctors back then to make sure it wasn't his lymph. But it was. The biopsy was to confirm that he had lymphoma.

Daniel was finally released from the hospital. I sat in the car and tried to figure out how we were going to celebrate Christmas. We had planned to go to Austin for Christmas Day to celebrate with my family at my parent's house. Daniel asked if we could go just straight there. I had planned to go back home and then go to Austin. But, understandably, he didn't feel up to it. It made sense to go straight to my parent's house. It would be less driving for him. I didn't know if my parents would agree to it and it was always so tense staying there. To my surprise, my mom told me to come and they would do whatever they could to help. My amazing eldest daughter went to work at home to make it happen. She gathered everything to make Christmas possible. If it were not for her dedication and determination, we would not have been able to celebrate Christmas that year. It was a lot to gather the gifts, the food, all the younger kids' clothes, and things. My phenomenal daughter was truly the hero that year, and made sure Christmas happened for us all, despite overwhelming challenges. Sadly, though surrounded by my parents and my sisters and their families, I did not feel welcomed or supported. They may have been physically present, but they were not emotionally available. I had always been the strong, encouraging one and I felt it was my responsibility as the oldest to watch out for them. But I couldn't this time. I needed encouragement. And yet I felt so alone. I just kept crying out to God, asking for divine wisdom, leading and guidance. I didn't understand how my own family couldn't support me. I went in the back room and sobbed because they completely left me out of parts of the celebration. It felt so cruel.

In the midst of all of this, I was having trouble sleeping in my bed again. I could sleep in the car, on the couch, in the bathtub, on the toilet, at the table, on the floor. I could sleep anywhere but the bed. I was tired of it. I wanted to find the underlying cause of it once and for all. I wanted freedom to sleep in my own bed. This had been happening for years.

Then I remembered when I was a student in college and had joined a Christian fellowship group called the Navigators. One night the speaker was talking about sexual abuse. It was the first time I had ever heard anything about it. In my family it was considered taboo to talk about sex at all. The women in my family acted like it was disgusting. The testimony shared by the speaker that night caused me to remember something that had happened to me when I was in first grade. I remembered it quite vividly. So, I gathered up my courage and reached out to one of the ladies there. What she told me left me stunned. She said she thought I had been sexually abused. *"What? How could this be?"* I thought. Like my son felt at his diagnosis, I was in disbelief. *"I had a good Christian family. That couldn't be abuse,"* I told myself.

Something stirred within me and I began reading everything I could. This was back before the internet, so reading was the best choice for me. I read one very pivotal book, *The Wounded Heart: Hope for Adult Victims of Childhood Sexual Abuse* by Dan Allender.

One of the things I remember telling myself the most is that, *"It wasn't that bad."*

I continuously denied my own pain around what had happened and who had done it to me. Finally, one day I decided to have a heart to heart with God about it. I talked with Him and He kept asking me if I really wanted to know. I kept saying, "YES!" Finally, the answer came, and it was devastating to me. I did a little more investigating and realized I had been molested in my sleep hundreds of times over the years starting in infancy. I will not go into any details of how I know, but it answered a lot of questions for me. It also brought up anger and so much grief. The pain and despair felt overwhelming. As a child, I didn't have the ability to navigate the emotions. I understood now why

I had so many sleep issues. That is why I was terrified of the monster coming to me. That is why I couldn't sleep in my bed. That is why I talked and yelled and even cursed at anyone who tried to wake me. This disruption had been going on my whole life. How could anyone do this to their child? How could you allow this to happen repeatedly to someone you love?

As I continued to press in and seek healing, I decided I had to go to my dad and talk to him about it. In tears, he said to me that he hoped I had forgotten, and he apologized. But my mom, she was angry and looked at me with hate in her eyes. It was one of the most awful feelings ever. My own mother denied me any comfort, validity, or support. I felt like I was the enemy. At that moment I thought she hated me. I didn't understand why she was so upset with me. Because of my deep Christian upbringing, I felt I couldn't share with anyone what had happened because it would dishonor my parents. I felt that was one of the worst things I could do. My faith was still strong, and I talked to God and prayed fervently for my mom and dad. I so desperately wanted my mom to love me unconditionally. I longed for her approval and attention.

I made up my mind that I would protect my children to the best of my ability. I would be their advocate, their protector, even if it meant not allowing them to spend much time with their only grandparents. I would stand by their side when it looked like they could die of cancer. Before we knew about Daniel's diagnosis, he had planned to volunteer for a week at a Boy Scout camp the day after Christmas. His older sister and younger brother planned to attend as well, and everyone was excited. When I told the oncologist of his plans, they said he couldn't go and participate due to the risks. But we had one week before any results would come back from the biopsy and before any treatments could begin, so I advocated for him to go. Did they want him to go home, curl up in a ball and be even more depressed? He couldn't receive any medical treatments during that time anyway. That oncologist was opposed, but reluctantly agreed to allow him to go. His sister and brother kept an eye out for him and helped him stay encouraged. The camp worked with us to allow him to have an easy job. They still talk about the memories they made at that camp! Personally, it was the best thing that could have happened for him to keep his mind busy after such devastating news.

Finally, the biopsy results came back, and it confirmed he had stage 4 Hodgkin Lymphoma. Daniel asked for another opinion and didn't want to start the treatment right away. What happened next was a shock to me. I got turned into child protection services for medical neglect. I was accused of refusing treatment. They accused me of saying things that Daniel had said. During those few days, I did so much research and no sleeping. I reached out to my holistic community as well. I finally found a doctor in Austin near my old elementary school and just a few minutes from my parent's house. It seemed as if we were being divinely led to Austin. The doctor I was trying to get Daniel in with suddenly had an opening early the next morning. I threw some things in the car and drove. It wasn't planned out; I just knew I had to get my son help immediately. My parents allowed us to stay there. I knew we needed to move to a bigger city because we needed to be closer to the treatment facility, so we didn't have to travel so many hours to receive treatment. Plus, Daniel needed to be in a bigger house. We had been living in an extremely tiny home following a devastating house fire. Daniel didn't have any space to withdraw for resting or healing. After doing many hours of research, I had Daniel's team in place. I began holistic treatments that supported Daniel emotionally, physically, spiritually, energetically. We coordinated with the oncologist who was aware of what I was doing. The holistic support I gave his body kept him from ever needing any more blood transfusions. His healing journey was on its way.

My daughter and I were preparing healing foods for him to support his body and help his body detox. We got him a yoga ball and a rebounder to get his lymph flowing. We were preparing food around the clock for him, giving him supplements and applying ointments and diffusing oils, playing healing music. We looked to create a healing environment in every way. At night, I would sleep in the twin bed with him to console him. He was too weak to go upstairs. Unfortunately, living with my parents was a very toxic environment for him and for all of us. It was killing Daniel. He was so weak he could not walk across the room without help, and he was constantly out of breath. He was a mere skeleton, and it was scary to see how thin he had become. I was afraid he would die. My mom yelled at him when he sat in a fetal position. She made faces at him behind my back and accused him of eating all kinds of sugary foods that did not support his healing journey. It was so stressful to everyone. I knew we couldn't go on like this. His weight had dropped to 112 pounds and he was 5'9".

I had a friend, an old college roommate in the north Dallas area reach out to me. She told me to move in with her. I was reluctant, but desperate. So, I went. Within two days of being there, my daughter called to tell me that she had just walked a mile with Daniel. I could not believe it! I remember asking her if she was sure because I was in such shock! It is amazing what a toxic environment can do to you and how much it can harm your health and well-being. Eventually everyone's health improved. Grayson was no longer allergic to sugar. I could eat and digest things that I had not been able to eat my whole life. Even though it was the most difficult valley I had ever been through, we had more joy. We left the abuse behind. And, our happy days outweighed the sad ones. Keeping my kids safe helped me keep myself safe. Protecting Daniel led me out of an abusive marriage. It was just me and my 7 kids going to every chemo infusion. Daniel was never alone at any infusion even though that decision caused me to get turned into child protective services again for medical neglect. Again, the case was dismissed. Advocating for my children, protecting my kids wasn't easy. It cost me. I left everyone I knew behind. I left the town I had known for 30 years. I cried many nights, alone. Yet, it was the best decision I ever made. I gained so much more.

Making the decision to get healthier, be healthier, stay healthier took sacrifice, commitment and meant not taking the easy way. It meant it was just God and me in the dark valleys. Being spiritual used to mean I stayed in abuse, put up with violence and kept silent. It meant everything looked like it was perfect. I did not do that on purpose. It was because I did not know any better. I thought loving God meant "dying" to myself, putting others first, honoring my parents and not speaking badly about people. I didn't realize by not speaking up I was allowing abuse to continue, that by keeping it hidden I was protecting the abuser and even allowing more victims. I thought that the trials I experienced meant I loved God more and I was just experiencing trials of many kinds like the Bible promised I would. I didn't understand that what I was experiencing was the opposite of God's love and His best for me. No one is meant to live in fear being abused. Loving yourself isn't selfish, ungodly, or evil.

Getting away from abusive relationships does not mean I didn't forgive the people or am giving up on relationships. It does not mean I do not love them or am a bitter person. It also does not mean I am a quitter, ungodly, unforgiven. It does mean that I value, honor, and love myself enough to get away from abusive relationships. It means that I protect myself and my kids, that I speak up and live in peace and harmony, free from violence. It means that I live authentically without hiding, perfectly imperfect, imperfectly perfect. It means I get to enjoy each moment and all the messy journeys, not just the destination. It means each day we choose to love ourselves, each other, and we live empowered and embrace our inner badass.

We are not victims of our circumstances.

Circumstances remind us of who we are.

We decide how we will react.

When we fall, we get back up.

We forgive ourselves, others and get back to love and support each other, honor each other and give grace and space to heal.

More About Melody:

Melody Self is a life coach, international best-selling author and award-winning public speaker. She created the Bad Ass Mamas Sisterhood Community to empower, encourage and educate women like you to get past your hurts, hang-ups, traumas and pains in a safe environment so that you can experience healing, health and wholeness, live your dreams and unleash your inner Badass.

Melody uses a variety of tools and methods inspired from her many certifications. She became a certified natural health professional, her first certification, as a result of her own health challenges. She has always loved educating and empowering others which led to her earning a bachelor and master's degree in bilingual education from Texas A&M University. She learned to speak, read and write Spanish in her mission to help others.

Melody is a Badass single mama to 7 amazing children, two girls and five sons, ages 7-21. She is a homeschooling mama of 15 years. Melody knows firsthand how unexpected life events cause stress and bring up trauma from a devastating house fire to helping her teen son through stage 4 cancer.

When she's not busy with her 'Selfs', you will find her enjoying nature, swimming in the lake, pool or beach, enjoying God's beautiful creation. She resides in north Dallas with her family. Connect with her on Facebook, Instagram or HealthySelfs.com and MelodySelf.com

The Gift You Share

by Julie D. Burch

> *The meaning of life is to find your gift. The purpose of life is to give it away.*
>
> ~ *Pablo Picasso*

It was going to be a crazy day. Maybe you have had one like this. I was scheduled to do a full day of training for a company in downtown Dallas. I live in a suburb of Dallas. So, it wasn't a long drive, but I knew there would be some serious traffic. I had to leave at the crack of dawn and fight the traffic all the way there. And I don't know why, but I get turned around and lost every time I drive to downtown Dallas! I finally get there, find a parking place, and do my training. I am a very high energy speaker, so when I speak all day, whew! I am tired. Now I am fighting my way through traffic back to my house and I am starting to get a little stressed. I am in a hurry because I am meeting my husband and grabbing my luggage so he can take me to the airport where I can catch a flight to Indianapolis, Indiana, then rent a car to drive an hour to Bloomington, Indiana so I can teach another full-day seminar the next day! And I am already exhausted. I am running late for my flight—fighting traffic to the airport—running through the airport to my gate—I am like OJ, jumping over chairs and stuff! I finally get to my gate and discover I am in a middle seat! We are changing planes in St. Louis, but all the way to St. Louis I am cramped in the middle. I finally get to St. Louis and my connecting flight to Indianapolis is delayed...4 hours. It is late, everything at the airport is closed, I am hungry, tired, and annoyed. We finally board the flight - I have a middle seat again, but at least we are on our way. I get to Indianapolis and it is now the middle of the night and I need to grab my luggage and go outside to catch the rental car shuttle. I walk outside and it is nine degrees below zero. Below. I didn't know it could go *below* zero! And y'all, I live in Texas. I don't know anything about cold weather. I wasn't even wearing socks!

So, I am standing there shivering, exhausted, and hangry waiting for the Alamo Rental Car Shuttle to come to pick me up. I am standing there watching every other rental car company go by—there was a Hertz, Avis, National, oh look another Hertz. I waited for twenty minutes! Finally, the shuttle arrives, I drag myself and my suitcase onto the shuttle bus and we're off. We pull up to the rental car center and, of course, it's the middle of the night, so I am the only customer there. I walk into this giant, brightly lit room, and all the way on the other side of the room there is one woman working. As soon as I am three steps in the building, from clear across the room she shouts, "Hi! How are you doing tonight?" My face automatically scrunched up into my best annoyed look, and I respond with a curt, *"Fine."* She looked right back at me and said, *"You don't sound fine."* Now my face twists right up into what can only be described as a combination of the devil and sheer shock. My tone was low, and the response was slow, but I heard myself say, *"Actually, I have had a long, exhausting day."* She didn't miss a *beat. She looked at me with a sweet and compassionate smile and said, "Then you have come to the right place!"* I stopped dead in my tracks. I looked around, stunned. Yep, I was still in the rental car center in Indianapolis in the middle of the night. I must have misunderstood her. Could she be serious? She continued, *"If you have had a long exhausting day, then exactly what you need is to get in a nice, comfortable car and go for a nice, relaxing drive!"* As soon as she said that I thought…oooh…relaxing drive, comfortable car, can there be music too? Can I have music? At that moment, she turned me around. She was kind. She was genuine. She was compassionate. And she wasn't about to let my snarly tone and ugly face change her disposition. Now, I was easy to turn around and not everyone is, but she made the effort. She made a difference in my life that night and I have never forgotten her. I don't know her name, but I call her Angel. She had a gift. And I was grateful that she shared it with me that night. Has someone ever shared their gift with you? Have you shared *your* gift with someone else?

Every heart has a gift. Every person has a gift. I believe that, and I'll bet you do, too.

Have you ever noticed how good we are at seeing other people's gifts? We can be just about anywhere and see the gifts of others. Have you ever looked around the room and thought *"I sure admire how confident she is?"* Or *"I love how smart she is?"* Or *"I admire her tenacity?"* I knew right away I admired Angel's gift of compassion and her positive attitude. We can be great at spotting other people's gifts and struggle to see our own. We tend to be so hard on ourselves. We tell ourselves all the time how bad we are at stuff. We will tell ourselves we are bad at everything from communicating to standing up for ourselves to raising our kids! That voice in our head loves to tell us all the bad stuff. My Mom taught me years ago that your subconscious can't take a joke!

It believes everything you tell yourself. So, when you tell yourself, I am bad at that, I have always been bad at that, you tend to believe it, it becomes a self-fulfilling prophecy. I have also discovered - and maybe it's just me - but once you have convinced yourself you are bad at something you have to justify and defend why you are bad at it. You will tell yourself *"I am just bad at it; I have always been bad at it. My Momma was bad at it too!"* Like it's genetic. It's not genetic! We must learn to see our value. We must learn to see our own gift.

For so many of us, this is all about our self-esteem. I know people shift in their chairs when we mention self-esteem. *Shhh… that's personal. We don't discuss such things with others*! Everyone needs to know that our self-esteem does matter, but it is more than that. Many years ago, I had it explained to me like this.

There are three parts to it: there is our self-esteem, our self-ideal, and our self-image. Our self-esteem is how much we like ourselves. Our self-ideal is us at our best. How we see ourselves in our ideal mind—us at our very best! Then our self-image is how we actually see ourselves behaving in everyday situations.

When your self-image does not live up to your self-ideal it lowers your self-esteem. For example, let's say your self-Ideal believes that you will always stand up for yourself. You defend yourself when you feel like you are being taken advantage of or personally attacked. Picture yourself in a meeting, you speak up and share your opinion and a coworker snaps at you and says something rude or sarcastic. You, in your ideal-self— you at your best self—would have responded assertively, calmly, and professionally. That would be you at your ideal self.

Now, if you don't respond appropriately, instead you shut down or make a face. You roll your eyes, attack back or say, *"Shut up, Frank!"* Then that is how you see yourself behaving in the situation. Now, when you leave that meeting, your self-image (how you behave) doesn't match your self-ideal (you at your best self), so your self-esteem goes down.

The opposite is also true. When you see yourself behave in a manner that is in line with your self-Ideal, your self-esteem goes up. We must *behave* in a way that is true to our ideal. We must see our value so we can LIVE our value. But most of us struggle a bit with seeing our value.

Let me give you a new way to think about it. I want you to think about someone you admire. A personal hero. They can be living or dead, someone you know personally, or someone you don't know personally. It can be someone from history or television. Who would you consider to be your personal hero? Write down their name. Trust me, just do it. It is important that you identify someone for yourself.

You might be thinking of your mom or your grandmother. Your favorite teacher or your aunt. So often, when I do this exercise in my seminars, I hear names like Oprah or Amelia Earhart. It can be anyone! Once you have your personal hero's name written down, write two to three traits or characteristics of that person that you admire. Not things they have accomplished in their life, but traits or characteristics they possess. For example, you wouldn't write that the person grew up poor and became successful, but rather you admire that they had tenacity or perseverance that helped them to be successful.

You might say that they had integrity, they persevered, they had a positive attitude, they were loving, they were hard workers, those would all be admirable traits. What traits does your hero have?

Here is the most amazing thing. Psychologists tell us the traits and characteristics you most admire in others are the traits and characteristics you yourself possess. I know, crazy, isn't it?

Whenever I share this, people respond with, "Oh no, not me," or," I wish I were like that." But it is true. You have a gift. I promise.

I learned this from my husband. He is amazing, I adore my husband. I still think of myself as a newlywed, so I still really like him a lot! I hear that may change. When I first started dating my husband 18 years ago, I described him as my rugged outdoorsman. He is a hunter, a fisherman, a camper, the outdoorsy type. And let's be serious, I was a city girl! But I was smitten! And smitten pretty darn quick. I knew he was the one! We had only been dating a couple of months when he told me he wanted to take me hiking to go deer scouting. I had no idea what that was! Some of you may know, this is when you go hiking in the woods looking for where the deer might be. I heard hiking and I knew that meant cute boots, so deer scouting we went! And I was excited to see some deer! We didn't see a lot of real deer in the city! So, out to the country we went! We hiked… and hiked… and hiked for miles! And the whole time, I kept saying *"where are the deer? I don't see any deer!"* And he kept saying "Shhhh!" I didn't know this little adventure required me to be quiet, and let's be honest, being quiet was not one of my strengths. He told me to be patient. Just because you don't see them doesn't mean they aren't there. You have to look a little deeper.

And he would point out all the clues that told us the deer had been there. He would show me the little hoof prints in the dirt and then tell me whether it was a buck or a doe. He could even tell me which way they had been walking. He pointed out the rubbings on the trees, and would say *"See, they were here!"* And I kept saying, "I don't *see them! Where are the deer? I want to see some deer."*

All day long we hiked and never saw one deer. That night, for the first time in my life, I slept in a tent on the ground. So, we woke up at the crack of dawn, because when you sleep in a tent on the ground, you will wake up at the crack of dawn. Trust me, the ground is not as comfortable as you might think. We were camping right on the edge of a lake, it was beautiful. I looked out the door of the tent and saw, standing just down the bank of the water, a whole deer family! A daddy deer, a mommy deer, and a little baby deer! I told my husband, "Look! Look! There they are!" And he calmly responded, *"I told you they were there. You just have to be patient. Dig a little deeper. Just because you don't see them at first doesn't mean they aren't there."* That was his gift to me. At that moment, I understood. He taught me that it is the same way with those traits and characteristics we admire. They are there. He helped me to see that, and I hope I can help you see it, too. Those traits are there. You may not see them at first, but just because you don't see them, doesn't mean they aren't there. Just like deer scouting, you have to be patient, you have to dig a little deeper. But *they are there*. Those are your gifts. When my Angel at the rental car center shared her gift with me, it changed my life. From that point on, I wanted to share my gift, too! I wanted to be someone else's Angel! You have the same ability, or, should I say, responsibility. You must share your gift with others. Because the best gifts are the ones we give away.

More About Julie:

Julie Burch is the President of Julie Burch Speaks, and in her over 20 years of speaking professionally, Julie has had the privilege of speaking to audiences in all 50 states, Washington DC, St. Thomas, St. Croix, Puerto Rico, Canada, England, and Wales. Where she has designed programs for industry leaders such as Texas Tech University, Fidelity Investments, Kaiser Permanente, CoServ Electric Cooperative, the Social Security Administration, the EEOC, Taco Bell, Texas Woman's University, Columbia Gas of Ohio, The American Payroll Association, The United States Army, The United States Air Force, Christus Health, Subway, Wingstop, Holiday Inn, Husky Oil, Armstrong Bank, American Advertising Federation, Armstrong Bank, BP America, and The Society for Human Resource Management.

Julie served as National Vice President on the National Board of Directors for the American Business Women's Association as well as on the Board of Directors for CYT- Christian Youth Theater of DFW. She was honored with a guest appearance on "Good Morning America" where she was interviewed by Diane Sawyer and was named the 2017 Speaker Hall of Fame Inductee at the Society for Human Resource Management's Southwest Conference.

Julie is the coauthor of two books including a motivational book for women titled *"The Princess Principle: Women Helping Women Discover Their Royal Spirit"* and *"Success Simplified: Simple Solutions Measurable Results."*

Julie is the comedienne with content! She has dedicated her life to the pursuit of helping companies improve the bottom line through strategic plans, consistent growth, and the development of people. She has coordinated, developed, and delivered top notch, highly effective classroom style training, web-based training, and motivational keynote presentations with powerful results. All of Julie's presentations are dynamic, high energy, highly interactive and packed with real world, tangible techniques the audience can implement immediately. Julie also loves to make them laugh! She has discovered the more her audience laughs the more they learn. "Solid Business Strategies. Brilliant Comedic Humor." It's not just her tag line, it is her promise in every presentation!

Contact Julie:

Website: www.julieburch.com
Email: julie@julieburch.com
Phone: 214.679.2717

The Gift of Faith

by Eva Diana Iguaran

> *For our wrestling is not against flesh and blood, but against the principalities, against the powers, against the world-rulers of this darkness, against the spiritual hosts of wickedness in the heavenly places.*
> ~ Ephesians 6:12 ASV

There we were, on the floor of our bedroom, both broken and desperate. I had never heard my husband weep like this. We had both been crying, grasping in the dark for some sort of answers. After some time, my husband said, *"just think how thoughtless we both were that one evening."*

When our daughter, Elianna, was younger, we had been enjoying an evening in our neighborhood park when suddenly, things took a turn for the worse. Elianna had been trying out the monkey bars. I was there, coaching her, but only half holding her. Suddenly, she fell to the ground. I was blaming myself, and she was blaming herself. There were tons of tears. Her dad and I started to have a conversation about her strength and her abilities - right in front of her. We stopped ourselves, realizing that she was right there, still crying over the whole ordeal. Somehow, a beautiful evening in the park turned into a sad memory, the guilt of our insensitivity now pulling at our heart strings.

This time, facing a nightmare situation, we tried to take a good look at what we were dealing with - this time, with two young children. I had no idea an issue this serious would ever enter our home, much less when our kids were so young.

Earlier that week, Elianna approached me with a face full of anguish. Thankfully, I had established a nightly routine of going to the kids' bedrooms to unwind and pray with them. That night was unusual because Elianna was extra talkative. I just sat with her and listened. She was in tears, bubbling out at a rate that I had trouble keeping up with. It was as though she had stored so many memories and thoughts that her brain could no longer hold it all in. Soon enough, we were both in tears. I reassured her that I had experienced similar thoughts, and I asked if we could talk with her dad about everything she had told me; I desperately needed another adult to hear what was on her mind. It was an exceptionally long night of talking, filled with more emotion than I had ever seen from her. She wanted so badly to get it all off her chest; I could not imagine how long these unresolved issues had been weighing on her small and fragile heart.

It was not until the next day that our family dropped into the longest tailspin of our lives thus far. Enrique and I never would have guessed that the next few weeks would call everything into question; we would have to hold on to our faith with every fiber of our beings.

That next day, Elianna came to me and fell to her knees at my feet. I tried pulling her to her feet, and she went limp. Enrique was at work - the only other person home with us was my son, Luisenrique. Elianna cried out, *"Mom, you don't love me!"* It was not one of those cries she would use to ask for some sort of treat, or gift. She needed my reassurance.

How could this be happening?

I loved her so much.

Everything I did was for her.

Everything!

In that moment, standing in our living room, I tried to comfort her. Later that day she came to me, saying that a voice had told her to kill herself. She had huge tears in her eyes. She whispered the words, and I almost wanted to question what I heard. These words cannot be coming from my eight-year-old daughter. I just held her, trying to process the seriousness of her words. The hours crept by as we waited for Enrique to get home from work. I told him, and we both were panicked about who to call, what to do. I called a friend of mine who was a social worker, and we decided we needed to get her to a doctor, fast. During that time, I kept that friend on speed dial, as she would help us greatly in the coming days.

A day later I was sitting at the kitchen table when Elianna came to me, crying, and told me that the voice told her to kill me and her dad. The situation was growing more intense. I had no idea what to say to that; once again, I just held her. It was like she just needed to get it off her chest, like a huge weight had been lifted. But now I was starting to fear my own daughter. I just loved on her, held her, and said it was going to be okay.

Finally, Enrique and I held each other and poured our hearts out in prayer, searching for answers. We did not trust anyone, but I was slowly making plans to handle this very delicate situation for which my husband and I were so unprepared.

I was scared to share this with anyone. I was scared for my life. There was a point in which I felt so paralyzed and scared that I was not sure I should even sleep. In fact, we got very little sleep for days. At least a week passed before I was able to get in touch with a professional. It may seem like we were too slow in our approach, but we were trying our best to figure everything out. There was one day that felt like one week. Throughout the day Elianna just cried and cried. The voice in her head was so loud; it seemed, to me, that she was dealing with a spiritual attack. I held her for what seemed like the longest hours ever. I was hurting for her because I myself felt paralyzed. It was pure torture. We rocked back and forth on her bedroom floor, me reminding her that I was there, repeating over and over, *"I'm here baby, I love you."* We were both sobbing uncontrollably. This was the darkest of days.

We finally got an appointment to see a doctor, and I was advised to speak with him as well. Elianna and I walked in together and sat in his office. He listened to me tell every part of the story. I did not leave off any detail from what she had told us or from what we had experienced.

He was calm, and very encouraging. Earlier that day I had been so scared that I was losing my daughter; now, he was telling me that at her age, her brain was still changing and that he did not recommend medication.

Many people may not agree with how we handled things, and I understand that. But I see now what a huge blessing this doctor was. I do not even want to think about what could have happened had I taken Elianna to the emergency room. It hurts deeply to even write this story now, considering some of the judgment I felt then, as well as reflecting on what happened versus all the what ifs. I was afraid Elianna would take her life. I was afraid she would take our lives. I was not afraid of her, but of Satan. There, I said it.

We left his office with no prescription to fill. I told him how she had spoken about all that was on her chest, all the words she heard spoken to her. How we were trying to figure those voices out together. I even told him about her being sick with fever a week prior to the events. Soon after, we had found a counselor to start seeing regularly. We both got to attend sessions, but at one point the sweet young lady would ask me to leave so she could see Elianna alone.

It was a strange time for us, but I felt like we were making progress. There were fewer outbursts, and we felt so much more hopeful. I wanted to tell my closest friends, but I did not. I was worried that even family members would be scared and judge us. I would eventually start to hint to family that Elianna needed a friend, but even with me dropping those hints, we felt all alone.

The fog of sleep deprivation and fear finally lifted. We had prayed, we had fought, and we had cried some more. We had loved our daughter all these years, but I was sure there were times we failed her in physically showing it. I understand now that we can love deeply and be fully committed, but at the same time not match that love and commitment in our words and facial expressions. I vowed to match the love in my heart on the outside. I made that promise, but it really is a decision I must remake daily; I must set that intention.

The last years have been full of both healing and learning. We have been open to change and have listened to the Holy Spirit. I believe God answered many questions I had at the time. One question that weighed on my heart: how and why was Elianna attacked at such a young age? It made no sense to me, considering how careful we had been with the choices we made for our family. I knew Elianna was innocent.

You may be familiar with the story of Akkin from the Bible Akkin had stolen goods hidden in the camp, and his whole family was punished for his actions. My warning to friends and family is to watch for "windows" or "doors" that could be left open without you knowing. The enemy just needs a small opening to create trouble in your home.

The adults in the home need to be aware of potential weak spots to prevent leaks. What starts small could turn into a flood. I later received confirmation and peace over what happened in our home. I am overwhelmed with praise because the enemy did not have his way with my family. We are now more faithful to our mission and we encourage others to fight the good fight and to be overcomers as well.

One thing I have learned is that what we watch and listen to can be an influence for good or evil. It is shocking how many children take their lives. In many cases it is a result of mental illness or a chemical imbalance, but there are also powers that seek to destroy. My family could feel and hear the evil in our home. I understand that this may be a very disturbing idea, but it is our truth - we lived it.

I feel blessed that we all lived to tell this story because I met a mother recently whose story did not have the same happy ending.

I am grateful to the doctor who said Elianna needed time and prayer, rather than medication.

I am grateful for a social worker friend who guided me through this time and reacted with love over judgment.

I am thankful to another friend who encouraged me to seek help immediately. The counselor gave us hope and pushed us to continue seeing her even when it was hard to even talk.

I am honored that Elianna is brave enough to allow me to tell her story.

I have been waiting for her to be old enough to give me consent to write about what happened; it is her story, even though we were also there. When she told me that she had finally opened up during a recent trip she took with her friends, I knew it was time.

This was a very lonely time because the topic is so stigmatized. I felt very scared to talk with anyone, and I even still find it difficult to share.

Mental illness is real.

Medication helps many who suffer. I am not a mental health professional, and I by no means wish for this story to promote the idea that it is always best to decline medication. I am, however, incredibly happy with the path we took; the choice we made was the right one for our family at that time.

More About Eva:

Eva Diana Iguaran is a professional birth videographer and photographer at Eva Diana Photography. She offers maternity, birth, and newborn sessions as her specialty but also does family, Seniors, and weddings.

She has attended over 100 births and many of her YouTube birth stories have gone viral. She has served clients such as Christine D'Clario and WePlusThreee.

Family is first for Eva Diana. That is why she loves her career. It is flexible with exception of occasional 2am births. She wants to see her children follow their God given talents and follow the dreams that set them on fire. She has homeschooled all three of her children through different grades and loves reading out loud and art the most.

Outside of work Eva Diana is pursuing becoming a triathlete. She pushes herself to be a better swimmer and cyclist. Running comes more natural for her. She recently completed a viral race across Tennessee of 635 miles of walking and running in 4 months. She loves adventure and wishes she could live in a tiny home and travel the globe. She has visited 15 countries. She also loves international cuisine.

Contact Eva:

Website: www.evadiana.com
Facebook.com/evadianaphotography

The Gift of Memories

by Cassie Pham Adams

> *What we have once enjoyed deeply we can never lose. All that we love deeply becomes a part of us.*
> ~ Helen Keller

They were soft and cozy navy-blue pajamas, made of 100% cotton, with warm long sleeves. She would have worn them for a chilly ski weekend, and I could picture her curled up on the sofa with a cup of hot cocoa in her hand. I had flown in from Los Angeles for the weekend, which I had been doing every other Friday. But this time was different; My mom called and told me to come as soon as possible. In my rush to leave town, I had forgotten to pack my own pajamas. Since visitation hours at the hospital were over, I went into the closet and searched for something to wear, simply grabbing the set of pajamas on the top of the stack. As I pulled the top over my head, I took in the fresh laundry scent. When I came out of the bedroom, my mom had a shocked look on her face.

"Why are you wearing those pajamas?" her voice shrieked, startling me.

"I didn't have time to pack anything to wear so I just borrowed these from her closet. What's the big deal?" I was confused by her reaction. My sister, Mindy, pulled me aside and told me in a quiet voice, *"These were the pajamas she was wearing when she had the stroke."* My heart dropped. Tears began to flow uncontrollably. *"Okay, I will go change,"* I said to my sister.

The pajamas belonged to my sister, Tess, who was battling lung cancer at the time. My mom had quit her job to become Tess's full-time caregiver and Mindy often came from England to help. When I said goodbye to my Tess 21 years ago, these pajamas were just one of three mementos I saved to remember her by.

She had a set of silky, luxurious lime green pajamas from Victoria's Secret, which was her choice for summer at home. I have memories of her wearing them, a beautiful color that paired perfectly with her long, dark and wavy hair. They were a size small, which is probably why she loved them. I remember her telling me one day about how she had lost a lot of weight in a short period of time due to her illness. She jokingly said, *"I finally got down to my driver's license weight, but what a way to get there!"* Those lime green pajamas take me back to our high school days, a casual reminder of sunny days, gymnastics, and our time together as sisters. I think of her every time I see them.

Tess loved dressing up. She always had way too many clothes, jewelry, and shoes in her tiny apartment. We used to share clothes growing up, and we would intentionally pack light whenever we visited each other, knowing we could borrow each other's clothes. When Mindy and I were sorting out the apartment after Tess passed away, I remember numbly packing everything into boxes. Mom had already returned to her home in Southern California, tired and defeated from the long ordeal. There were so many things from Tess I wanted to keep and cherish, but we decided to donate most of her belongings to charity. The one item I knew I must hold onto was her silver bangle bracelet with tiny circles all around. It was modern yet elegant, and a perfect reminder of Tess. I packed it for myself and kept it.

In the many years following Tess's passing, every time I visited a new place, I wanted her to enjoy it with me. When I traveled, the first things I placed in my suitcase would be the bracelet and one of the pajamas, depending on the weather at my destination. It seemed silly but the packing ritual made me think of Tess in present tense, like *"what would Tess have worn?"* I also did this so we could continue to share life's special moments and adventures.

We had enjoyed so many beautiful experiences together, from my first visit to San Francisco to an impromptu trip to Virginia for a tax-free weekend shopping spree! We took our first trip to Paris one Christmas, and I remember losing track of time in town and having to hitchhike to catch the last train back home. Tess came to visit me once on my first business trip, and we ended up buying bathing suits so we could swim in the hotel pool that night. We also enjoyed an amazing trip to New York together, complete with a visit to the Metropolitan Museum of Art, which culminated with us sitting on the front steps of the building eating a salted pretzel. She even surprised me with tickets to see the Broadway show "Cats," which was my first time seeing a live show in New York. We had plans to travel to Disney World when Tess called me to share the news of her cancer diagnosis. At the time, I truly thought she would make it. She maintained a positive mindset the entire time, in spite of the pain. Having a positive attitude is now one of the traits I now try to emulate in my own life.

I used to have many flashbacks to my short time with Tess. Whenever I missed her, I would put on her blue pajamas at bedtime and think back to our time together. I did not want to let go of her three things I kept for fear of losing my memories of her.

I thought about the conversations with her friends I met at her funeral, learning she was a dedicated volunteer at the hospital in the neonatal unit. This was news to me. Perhaps she was aware that hospitals made me really uncomfortable, or how I was afraid of blood.

After the funeral, I was determined to honor her life by continuing her path. I even looked into volunteering at a nearby hospital but never followed through. That fact continued to haunt me until one day a dear friend commented exasperatedly, *"You don't have to live your life for Tess. Go live your own life!"* This was so liberating, and I absolutely needed to hear it. Around that time, my sister Mindy became pregnant, and I learned to sew baby quilts to give as gifts. I ended up making five extra quilts and donated them to the hospital's neonatal unit. The day after the quilts were delivered, I held those blue pajamas in my hands for several minutes before packing them into a box with old clothes to donate to charity. I felt peace in how I had honored Tess's memory and was able to let the pajamas go.

The most precious gift I received from Tess was the lesson to live life purposefully. I ended up volunteering more often after that, by leading the Secret Santa program for the city and helping run the free bike parking lot at the beach in the summer for many years. I even started an annual Phamily grant for my twelve nieces and nephews, most of whom Tess never had the chance to meet. When I read the essays they submitted as part of the grant, I thought of how proud Tess would have been.

The silky green pajamas and silver bracelet were deeply tied to joyful memories of Tess, so I continued packing them in my suitcase for many more years. Anytime I would stay at my mom's house, I would wear the green pajamas so Tess could be part of our family conversations. I did not tell anyone they belonged to Tess. As time passed, my need to bring them on every trip would lessen, and eventually I only brought them on international trips or special occasions. They remained safely in my closet the rest of the time.

I still cherish that beautiful silver bracelet, which sits prominently on top of my modest jewelry collection. It accompanied me on my most recent trip to Arizona with Mindy.

I have heard the saying so many times that *"time heals all pain."*

But does it?

Is twenty-one years long enough to grieve a loved one?

No matter where the navy blue pajamas, silky green pajamas or silver bracelet may be, I have made a decision. Tess is forever with me in my heart and the bond we shared became part of who I am today. I have the memories stored safely there, and I am now ready to travel lighter on my own journey.

More About Cassie:

Cassie Pham is a full-time analyst in the corporate world who has a passion for writing short stories with an Asian folktale twist. More recently, she finds joy in building a community of friendship to help promote health and wellness. She is happily married to her husband and fellow cyclist, Corey, who shares her interest in exploring life on the pedal. They live in North Dallas, Texas.

Contact Cassie:

Email: cpham2008@gmail.com

The Gifts in the Call to Rise

by Sherri Elliott-Yeary

> *Drum sounds rise on the air, and with them, my heart. A voice inside the beat says, I know you are tired, but come. This is the way.*
>
> ~ *Rumi*

My world was crashing down, so I decided to take a three-week sabbatical to Cancun. This was the first time I had taken a trip by myself, for myself. One sunny afternoon I was feeling restless, so I grabbed my purse and strolled through a local flea market. As I wandered deeper into the market, I came across an alleyway lined with shops selling religious artifacts. Normally I would veer away from these kinds of stores, but I was seeking inspiration and healing on this trip. I didn't know where or how I was going to discover it, but I knew it was out there.

One narrow, dusky shop appealed to me, and I went in. A patchwork of rugs was arranged on the floor. Small paintings on wood hung on the walls. Was this a gallery, a rug store or a gift shop? I couldn't tell. In the back of the room two women sat dressed in muumuus, the kind my mom wore. One was older and the other might have been her daughter or niece. The younger woman had hypnotic green eyes and long flowing chestnut hair. After what seemed like forever, the older lady put down her tea and came forward to greet me. Fixing her gaze on me, as if trying to read the secrets of my soul, she said in perfect Spanish, *"Come, you will like this picture."* Taking me by the hand, she led me around piles of rugs to the very back of the store where her husband was sitting. The elderly gentleman stood and shuffled over to meet me. He placed his hand on his heart and bowed his head in respect.

"Look," he said, pointing to a small painting on the wall. He gently touched my arm with the kindness of a grandfather. *"See the rose?"* he asked, turning me toward the picture. There, framed in dark wood was the ethereal image of a rosebud, with shimmering pale petals holding one another in a loving embrace. Under the flower in small letters was an inscription that read:

> *And the time came when the risk to remain tight in a bud was more painful than the risk it took to blossom.*
> ~ *Anais Nin*

Unexpected tears stung my eyes as I read the words. The ladies hovered over me, more like guardian angels than salespeople. I quickly turned away from them, hiding my face behind my scarf. I was afraid if any of them showed me an ounce of kindness I would break down right there in this stranger's store, hundreds of miles away from home.

"What is wrong?" the younger lady asked.

"Nothing is wrong," I replied. *"I'm fine."*

"No, something is upsetting you," the lady replied. *"You look like your heart is broken and you are lost."*

"What do you mean?" I inquired, even though I was pretty sure why she asked.

As I turned away from them, hiding my tear stained face in the shadows, she answered, *"I can see you are in deep sorrow and your inner light has been dimmed."*

"What do you mean exactly?" I asked.

I wondered if these ladies had psychic powers and could see into my soul or were attempting to make a sale. Was my pain and heartache that obvious, my broken heart so easily read? I felt naked and exposed under their gaze, as if the older lady had a direct link to my soul and knew all about the loss of my marriage, my home, and my daughter's drug relapse after being clean for over eight years.

All I wanted to do was buy the painting and get out from under their kind gazes because I was not sure if I could keep it together much longer. This trip was meant to be a break away to reflect and grieve the loss of my marriage, and here I stood on the verge of tears, talking to complete strangers.

I quickly purchased the painting and as they wrapped it for me, the young woman with the chestnut hair wrote on the receipt, *"Your heart is like a flower, let it break open and it will show you what you want is waiting for you in your own heart."*

Then, she slipped to the back of the store where I could no longer see her. I walked out of the door with my painting secured under my arm as I stepped into the beautiful sunshine and wound my way back to my hotel. I was still feeling restless, so I changed into my bathing suit and headed to the beach for an invigorating swim in the ocean. As I swam, I kept picturing my heart like a rosebud, fused together, tight and tense, terrified to open.

This symbolized my fear of opening my heart.

Yet I knew it was time for me to do the work that I had avoided for too long. I gifted myself the time to vulnerably open the wound and heal the dark places of my soul. Even if I was risking all of me, the lady was right: It was time to find out what I really wanted, not what anyone else wanted. This was the time for me to bravely step into the fullness of life, with all its dangers and all its promises. I was no longer satisfied staying closed like the rosebud. It was time to blossom.

How strange that the nature of life is change, yet the nature of human beings is to resist change at all costs. And how ironic that the challenging times we fear might shatter us into a million pieces, are the very ones that prepare us for who we are meant to be.

You may be at the beginning of a transition, feeling only a vague mood of agitation or an intense calling in the direction of something new. Or perhaps you are in a full-blown period of change; what you thought your life was supposed to be has ended and your future is now uncertain. Perhaps you are coming out of the woods from a difficult period with your spouse or your career, and you can finally take a breath and make sense of the journey. Or maybe you have become aware, once again, of the obvious yet startling fact that nothing stays the same for long. You realize that things like your body, relationships, children, and work, are fluid and fleeting.

When you can no longer stand the pain and discomfort of life, that's the signal that it's time to step back and reflect on the real causes for your feelings. Like the rose in the painting, blooming equates to personal growth. Choosing growth over fear can be difficult, but the rewards are long lasting. When you approach life's challenges with openness and vulnerability, as I have, you can grow into a more fulfilled place in your life.

Whenever I feel the tug at my heart that indicates something is wrong, I know my heart is signaling me to bravely step into a new awareness and do the work necessary to receive the gift of healing. I have experienced many dark nights of the soul, when I knew deep in my heart that the pain would pass. My responsibility in those times was to take the next right step. When life is so overwhelming and hard, I've found that I need to take small actionable steps to get through a crisis or past trauma.

When my daughter started using methamphetamines again, I didn't think I would ever stop crying, let alone smile. By taking inspired action daily, I slowly started to heal and get stronger with each choice. I was not going to let fear win. My personal motto is *"Do it afraid."*

Overcoming Life's Challenges

It would be impossible to delve into all the reasons for suffering. Instead I want to focus on what I did to rise from the ashes. I went on a deep journey inside myself, honestly assessing what caused my angst and pain.

Many of us feel uncomfortable revealing to others and even to ourselves what lies beneath the surface of our day-to-day consciousness. We get out of bed in the morning and begin again where we left off yesterday, attacking life as if we were waging a campaign of control and survival. All the while, deep within us flows an endless river of pure energy. It sings a low and rich song that hints of joy, liberation and peace. On the surface, as we make our way through life, we may sense the presence of the river. We may feel a subtle longing to connect with it. But we are usually moving too fast, feeling distracted, or we fear disturbing the status quo of our surface thoughts and feelings. It can be unsettling to dip below the familiar and descend into the more mysterious realms of the soul.

I use the word soul because I have found no other word that better describes the river of energy that animates who we are. I have heard this river of energy called the life force, consciousness, or God, but I prefer soul because of the way it sounds.

You may not be able to hold it in your hands, but the soul is real.

If you are in the habit of negating the desires of the soul, the idea of it makes you nervous, or if you regard the subject with raised eyebrows, you may want to consider Rumi's advice:

> *When you do something from your soul, you feel a river moving in you, a joy.*

If you already understand what Rumi is talking about, I believe that you are in touch with your soul. And, if his words bring up sadness, cynicism or anxiety, I believe your soul is sending you messages;

messages that hopefully you will examine so you can move forward on a better path.

Your soul is always sending you messages.

If you regularly paint, sing, write poetry, listen to uplifting music, meditate and pray, walk in nature, or move your body in sports or dance, you know what it feels like when you and your soul are connected. You feel a river moving you to inspired action.

Yet so often we resist the pull of the soul and tune out its call. Perhaps we fear what the soul would have to say about choices we have made, habits we have formed, and decisions we are avoiding. Perhaps if we quieted down and asked the soul for direction, we would be moved to make big changes.

Throughout my life, in my journey through crisis to healing, I've found key actions that allow me to move through something, to rise from the ashes. I've described these key actions below.

Release Grief

When you go through a tragedy like the loss of a relationship, death of a loved one, or loss of a job, in order to move forward you must first accept the situation and allow yourself the grace and time to grieve. Why? Tragedy always creates strong emotions. If you do not release them, they will work against you and fester.

Did you feel any strong emotions this week? You may not always know what to do with your feelings. If you do not deal with them, but instead stuff them deep, your recovery from a crisis will take far longer than it should. Daily journaling is key for discovering what your body and heart are trying to tell you. Something magical happens when you put pen to paper.

Some people are stuffers, like I used to be. If I can avoid feeling the feelings, I usually try that first, even when I know from experience it does not work. When we experience painful emotions that we are not sure how to handle, we may deny, ignore and stuff them down instead of trying to deal with them.

Grieving what you have lost is an important first step of the healing process. Even though it's painful, face your feelings, do not repress them by pushing them down or rehearse them by repeating them over and over. Release your emotions with a coach, therapist, or good friend. If you do not talk it out, you will end up taking it out on yourself or someone you love.

Receive from Others

When you are hurting it is natural to want to hide and isolate yourself from others, especially when you are in the middle of a crisis. Even if you want to be alone during a difficult period, it's fine to rest, but once you have, make sure to reach out to a friend who can offer you unconditional love and support. You need their perspective, support, encouragement, and their presence.

If you are a person who is always in charge and has it together, it may be hard to receive from others or ask for help. Many times, people are blessed when someone asks them for help. During life's struggles, there is nothing wrong with asking for help and receiving from others.

Refuse to Be Bitter

Over the years, one of the things I've learned from coaching other women is the fact that there is absolutely no correlation between your life experiences and your happiness. I've seen people who lived through absolutely the worst experiences in life—things that would shock you, and yet they maintain a happy, cheerful, positive attitude, because happiness is a choice. In my coaching practice I have seen people who had every right in the world to whine yet chose not to do so. Happiness was their choice.

You can choose to be better or bitter, the choice is yours. If you allow yourself to stay stuck in bitterness, those toxic emotions and energy can manifest in your body as illness. Blaming someone else for your pain will not help you feel better; it only makes you feel worse.

How do you keep from being bitter when the inevitable tragedies of life happen?

- You accept what cannot be changed.
- You focus on what is left and be thankful for what you have and not what you have lost.
- You look inward and practice self-love.

Remember What is Important

Disasters have a way of clarifying our values and pointing out what matters and what no longer serves us.

Please do not confuse your net worth with your self-worth. A wise friend advised me not to judge my outsides based on everyone around me. I used to believe if I looked good on the outside, no one would be looking at my insides. Do not confuse your possessions with your purpose in life. Don't confuse what you're living on with what you're living for. Your life does not consist of what you possess. Relationships are what matters. You are never going to see a hearse with a U-Haul behind it, so build your life around something that can never be taken from you.

Can you lose a home? Yes. Can you lose a career? Yes. Can you lose a marriage? Yes. Can you lose your health? Yes. Can you lose your youthful beauty? Yes. But you have choices for how you grow from these challenges. These types of life-altering situations present an opportunity to choose the right actions to help you move forward.

Fill Your Own Toolbox

When I find myself broken and unable to move through a difficult period in my life, that is usually when my personal toolbox is empty. When what worked in the past no longer works, so I take the time to explore and implement new methods of healing in my life. Suffering and tragedy transform us, humble us, and bring out what matters most in life.

So, if you are going through a difficult time and what you have done in the past isn't working, find a new way to deal with what you are going through. Perhaps in the past you have talked to certain friends to help you through a crisis, but now those friends are not in a place to help you. You might have to work through your situation with a professional coach or counselor.

I hope that these ideas will help you walk through your life on a deeper and richer path. Painful situations in your life should not be ignored. Everything requires your attention. You can discover spiritual gems from the difficult challenges you face.

In the words of Chesborn Hanefesh, *"By failing to accept your suffering, the pain you feel will be much more acute and harsh."*

When circumstances seem the worst, you still have choices. Walking through trauma or tragedy, even when the road is peppered with obstacles, you can triumph, rise above and learn from the situation.

Our stubborn egos are knocked around, and our frightened hearts are broken open, not once, not in predictable patterns, but in surprising ways and for as long as we live. The promise of being broken and the possibility of blossoming like the rose are written into the contract of human life.

Certainly, this unbridled journey on the waves can be tiresome. When the sea gets rough, and when you are suffering, you may want to give up hope and give in to despair. But brave pilgrims have gone before you, they tell you to venture forth with faith and courage.

More About Sherri:

Sherri Elliott-Yeary is the leading expert on the impact of generational change and its impact on the workplace. As an author, columnist, blogger, and lecturer, she imparts a clear understanding of how generational demographics are changing the landscape of business. Sherri and her consulting firm, Generational Guru, have provided research and consultation on generational issues to hundreds of companies and professional groups, ranging from small businesses to multinational corporations, as well as major professional associations, for over 15 years.

Sherri Elliott-Yeary is a storyteller and a lover of words. She shares her own personal stories to lift our spirits, open our hearts, and offer us ways to create greater meaning in our lives. The driving force of her life and her work is the deep desire to live a life of meaning, while growing spiritually and serving others.

All of Sherri's offerings, coaching, motivational speaking, and training programs, are based on her personal journey and explore how we can come together and co-create a deeper sense of meaning in the world.

Contact Sherri:

Websites:
www.generationalguru.com or www.zensualgal.com.
Instagram.com/sherrielliottyeary
YouTube: Sherri Elliott-Yeary
facebook.com/sherri.elliottyeary.5

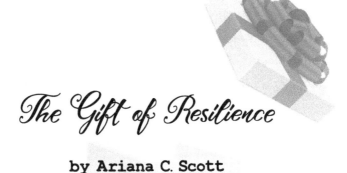

The Gift of Resilience

by Ariana C. Scott

I am Themis. I must maintain balance, the burdens of pain and pandemic trying to tip my scales. With Gaia as my guide, I begin to navigate this time of birth, death, and rebirth that has engulfed our earth. I stumble forward - unprepared, but not unsupported - Time on my side and sword at the ready. I must protect our Fates, but my Oracle now rests with Apollo, and I won't fly that close to the sun. Blindfolded - but not blinded - I push forward, equipped to lacerate the lies.

Honest does not always mean easy to understand.

Authenticity is not just telling the truth.

It is telling the truth and telling *your* truth.

It is walking (and sometimes sprinting) through hate-fueled fire.

It is floating between the black and white and then realizing that every line is gray

and then deciding that no, that isn't true - some lines are gray and others are very much black or very much white (good luck identifying which lines are which) and quite a few just absolutely should not be crossed (but some should be crossed because some rules are made to be broken).

Dancing in my truth has been difficult and painful, as if I'm a ballerina and the high road is a new pair of pointe shoes I just can't seem to break in without burying my body in blisters. Painful as it is, I stand tall through the pain and I count my blessings.

ONE

month since my fiancé passed, but not a day goes by in which I don't see him because he left me the most perfect gift, and it has almost been

TWO

months since our beautiful daughter - who looks just like him - joined us earthside. She has helped me heal, her calm energy grounding me at

THREE

o'clock in the morning, when the weight of my situation feels heavier than anything I've ever been forced to carry.

Some days I am Atlas.I look down at the gorgeous girl who has stolen my heart, and I know everything will be okay. The weight of the world seems significantly more carriable because *she* is my world.

And like the powerhouses atop Mount Olympus, we will overcome.

More About Ariana:

Ariana is a freelance graphic designer and social media influencer, specializing in helping small businesses and entrepreneurs create cohesive branding images and content. She graduated from Louisiana State University in 2019 with a Bachelor of Arts in English, with a concentration in Rhetoric Writing, and Culture. She is a single mom to Rémi Morgan, born July 9, 2020. Her fiancé, Norris Stevenson passed away unexpectedly shortly after their baby girl was born. She currently resides in Carrollton, Texas.

Contact Ariana:

Website: labellabyari.com
Facebook: facebook.com/labellabyari/
Instagram: instagram.com/arianacscott

Have You Received the Calling to Become an Author?

- Do people often tell you, "you need to write a book!"

- Do you have a way with words or just love to write?

- Do you have a message that needs to be shared with the world?

- Have you wanted to publish your story but are overwhelmed by the editing and/or formatting options and steps?

Join us for our next book, **Every Heart Has a Voice**, scheduled for release in fall 2021.

We are searching for stories from women all across the world to fill the pages of our book with inspiration, encouragement, motivation, and heart.

Visit our website at everyheartproject.com/collaboration to sign up as an interested author, and you'll be the first to know when applications open!

We cannot wait to hear your powerful story.

Made in USA - Kendallville, IN
1169809_9798682241293
09.24.2020 0833